Presented To:

_____

From:

_____

Date:

_____

THE ART OF
PRESENTATION

THE ART OF
PRESENTATION

YOUR **COMPETITIVE** EDGE

RAY HULL, PhD
& JIM STOVALL

TO CLAIM YOUR ADDITIONAL FREE RESOURCES
PLEASE VISIT soundwisdom.com/jimstovallbooks/

Cover design by Eileen Rockwell
Interior design by Terry Clifton

For more information on foreign distribution, call 717-530-2122.

Reach us on the Internet: www.soundwisdom.com.

Sound Wisdom
P.O. Box 310
Shippensburg, PA 17257-0310

ISBN 13 HC: 978-0-7684-1139-3
ISBN 13 TP: 978-1-9378-7958-7
ISBN 13 Ebook: 978-0-7684-1140-9

For Worldwide Distribution, Printed in the U.S.A.
1 2 3 4 5 6 7 8 / 20 19 18 17

CONTENTS

FOREWORD

One of our greatest fears has been found to be the fear of standing on stage and speaking before an audience. That doesn't seem possible, but numerous studies over the years have concluded that the fear of public speaking is frequently even greater than the fear of heights, snakes, drowning, flying, ghosts, and even death!

This book is written to address the various elements involved in effective presentations that are understandable and usable. They are broken down so that if you follow them you can become a presenter who, although still nervous, can "wow" your audiences rather than bore them. On the other hand, we must understand that not everyone is designed to be a dynamic speaker. However, although perhaps not possessing the dynamics and delivery of a Martin Luther King, we can be the best public presenter we are capable of becoming.

The elements that comprise the content of this book, among others, are as follows:

1. Stage fright and why people experience that awful moment when fear takes over and the words that were rehearsed for one's presentation fail to come forth. Our greatest fear involves standing in front of an audience unable to speak!

2. Why we fear presenting before an audience and how to overcome that fear.

3. What comprises a great presenter? What do they have that I don't?

4. Who are the great speakers who have changed the world?

5. Who are the speakers who are capable of influencing one's life and career?

6. The ingredients of a great public presentation—speaking tips and techniques.

7. The art of preparing a winning presentation. What do those presentations contain, and

how do I construct one for myself? How do I know if I am doing it correctly?

8. Delivering a presentation that will "wow" the audience. How do I organize my presentation so that the audience will applaud when I conclude it?

9. Who are the poorest public speakers? What are the ingredients that can result in a poor public presentation?

10. The art of using a microphone. Microphones are not our enemy, nor do they bite!

11. The art of stage presence and the manner of our presentation. What makes a great public presenter who is able to "own their audience"? How does that happen?

12. The art of concluding a presentation. In order to make an impact on your audience, the conclusion is just as important as the beginning of a great presentation and sometimes even more so!

13. Public speaking in your business and your life.

This book is written with those elements in mind and is constructed in a way that is easy to read and easy to understand. It is written to help you, the reader, to gain the confidence that you need to be the very best presenter you are capable of becoming. We want you to "wow" your audience so that they will want more, not less. We want you to be the best "you" that you are capable of becoming when you stand before an audience with a microphone in your hand. You have that potential, or you wouldn't be reading this book!

RAY HULL, PhD and JIM STOVALL

CHAPTER ONE

PUBLIC PRESENTATIONS AS A PERFORMING ART

By Ray Hull, PhD

Presenting is an art form—an art form that is created by you. You are the artist and the performer. The performance that you create—the scenery, the picture that you evoke with your words, touching the heart and soul of those who receive it—is your audience. They are the ones who will evaluate your creation, just as any art form is evaluated by those who view it or, in this case, listen to it.

Presenting in public is an art form because it comes from you, an individual who possesses your own individual style. You create the stage, the scenery, and the characters as you envision them, not as someone else would envision them. The stage and the characters are ones that you and only you create—that will make it a great performance. You are the artist, so you have the opportunity to make your creation one that will move your audience to a standing ovation, not one that puts it to sleep! It is not a performance that you are copying from someone else. It has to be authentically *you*, the author and creator of your own art form. And we don't want to be someone we are not. We want to be our own creative self, because it is *me* who is the artist, the one who is creating this masterpiece!

However, we do not want our performance to be a reckless one, to "show off," or to "stage act." Rather, our performance must be one that is well prepared; we must learn about the elements that will give us the confidence to be the best public presenter that we possibly can be. On the other hand, it must also be creative and inspirational.

Why Are There So Many Poor Public Presenters?

Why are so many public presenters so poor at what they do? I find it interesting that among the poorest public speakers I have had the misfortune to experience are those who are pastors who give sermons to their congregations on Sunday morning, politicians who are striving to obtain an important political office, professionals who speak at state and national conferences and conventions to inform us of the results of their research, or invited speakers who present their opinions on important subjects. One would think that individuals in important positions would speak in such a way that we would not have to struggle to hear and understand what they are saying.

What are the primary problems that prevent audiences from hearing and understanding what they are saying? They include, among others: 1) the fact that they are speaking at speeds that exceed the human central nervous system's ability to comprehend spoken speech; 2) when speech is spoken at high rates of speed, it becomes impossible for speakers to form the sounds of speech within individual words that allow for them to be articulated as whole words that in turn form sentences; 3) the microphone is misused—that is, the speaker does not know how to use a microphone so that it is allowed to perform as it should; 4) the speaker is obviously not prepared to speak in an organized and confident way, and 5) many other problems that prevent pubic speakers from being as good as they might otherwise be.

This Chapter

This chapter provides information on public speaking as a performing art. It is presented in such a way that the next time you are asked to speak on stage before an audience, you will not reveal the difficulties that so many others have when they are handed a microphone and asked to "Please say a few words to the audience."

Whenever I am asked to present before an audience, I freeze! Most people I have spoken with call it "stage fright." Why do I become so frightened?

Researchers from Chapman University conducted a survey on "American fears," which examined fears and anxieties that Americans frequently reveal across a variety of scenarios including fear of bugs, snakes, walking alone in the dark, death, clowns, vaccinations, ghosts, drowning, and others. They even compared fears and anxieties between political parties, but that is not the topic that we are discussing here.

It is interesting to note that significantly greater than the fear of heights, bugs and snakes, drowning, falling from a great height, vaccinations, claustrophobia, flying, zombies, darkness, ghosts, and even death is the fear of speaking in public! This phenomenon has been discussed for many years, but good research in that area has not really substantiated this phenomenon before. In one survey, people were simply asked to name, off of the top of their head, some fears that they have.

The interesting finding is that more of them mentioned speaking in public than death. According to Chad Schultz,[1] this would seem to imply that speaking in public is something that is more presently pressing on people's minds. In other words, people may be actively fearing public speaking more than they actively fear death because presenting a speech may be something they are facing currently rather than in the future.

Why Do People Fear Speaking in Public?

Whatever the reason, it is interesting and revealing that people actively fear speaking in public—that is, holding a microphone near their mouth and standing before an audience on a stage to give a presentation. Why? Probably one of the major reasons is that when a person is standing on a stage holding a microphone so that everyone can hear all of their words clearly, they have found themselves in the uncomfortable position of being absolutely vulnerable to everyone in the audience—their ability to speak, their manner of dress, their choice of words, their poise, their mannerisms while on stage, and more. That is, they are at the will of the audience that will appraise them and judge them in their own time and in their own way. That does tend to make those who have had little or no experience speaking in public feel quite vulnerable.

One of my most embarrassing moments involved one of my first attempts at speaking in public. Except in this instance, I was speaking before my friends in a high school classroom. At that time, I was a severe stutterer and was unfortunately *required* to take a course during the fall semester of my junior year in high school entitled "Public Speaking 110." On the first day of class, our teacher asked each of us, in turn, to stand beside our desk and introduce ourselves and tell about something that we did during the summer.

As each student's turn came and she or he stood by their desk, gave their name, and fluently told of an adventure or some amusing event that they experienced during the previous summer, I became increasingly nervous. Being a severe stutterer, I could not remember speaking a complete sentence to anyone, let alone speaking before a classroom of students who were my peers. The worst part of the situation was that they all knew me, knew that I stuttered, and knew that I would "fall apart" when it came to be my turn. As the students behind me told the class their name and told the story about their summer and my turn drew nearer, my throat began to tighten, my face began to become rigid, I blushed, and then I panicked!

When it was my turn, I stood beside my desk and started to say, "My name is…." But all that I could utter was "Ma…ma…ma…ma…ma…" trying desperately to say "My name is." I finally quit trying and sat down at my desk with my face in my hands, trying not to look at the other students. I heard quiet snickering among them, and the teacher simply said, "Uh...thank you Raymond," and went on to the next student who spoke with confidence and fluency. I was terribly embarrassed that I had done this to myself! I knew that I would not be able to speak in public, but I was required to do just that. My teacher required it, and I had failed. Public speaking terrified me, and I had let it embarrass me in front of my classmates!

I had experienced a true moment of stage fright. I never wanted to place myself in that situation again. But throughout that semester, I had to give prepared speeches before the class. And each time I prepared one and gave it, interestingly enough I became more fluent. By the tenth presentation that semester, I was nearly fluent and became aware that I was almost enjoying the experience of standing before my audience (my public speaking class) and presenting a speech! Practice makes perfect, as they say, and in this case it was working!

By the time I had graduated from college and was a professional in the field of communication sciences and disorders, I was speaking fluently and was becoming a sought after public speaker on the topic of "The Art of Communication." I had reached a point in my life when I was truly enjoying getting up before an audience and attempting to "wow them" with what I had to say. In order to break the ice with an audience and to give me a sense of balance as I stand on stage, I usually say, "I have truly looked forward to being here, and I know I will enjoy talking with you!" Then

I say with enthusiasm, "Give me a stage, a spotlight, a good microphone, and an enthusiastic audience, and I'm a happy boy!" And I say it with conviction, not anticipation and fear! I mean it! I know that it sounds rather self-serving, but it works, and it helps to warm up the audience—and me!

The Problem and the Solution

The problem with presenting in public, however, is that we, for better or for worse, are exposing ourselves to an audience, no matter how large or small, who can independently pass judgement on us and our ability to present ourselves before them, on what we say, and on how we say it. But with experience, we can develop tougher skin and get over that feeling of vulnerability. Remember, one way or another, we do survive!

As I said in the book *The Art of Communication*, we all become nervous before going on stage to speak. Being nervous helps us to remain on top of our game. If we aren't nervous, we probably won't do our best job. Remember, you are only as good as your performance, and public speaking is, again, a performing art. And we won't perform to our best ability unless we are nervous to at least some degree. As Mark Twain once said, "There are two types of speakers, those who are nervous, and those who are liars." I have heard actors admit that if they ever find themselves not being nervous before a performance, it is time to quit.

I want to be a great presenter of speeches. So what are the characteristics of those who present well? What do I have to do in order to be one of those?

I recall attending sessions of a Dale Carnegie public speaking course when I was a senior in high school. It was part of my attempt to rid myself of my stuttering without actually having speech therapy. One evening we were each to give a ten-minute speech on a topic that might be of interest to the rest of the group. I don't think that any in that Dale Carnegie course that was comprised of a mixture of working or soon to be working professionals, along with some high school and college students, were interested in what any of the rest of us had to say as we spoke before the rest of the class. Everyone was so nervous that I doubt that any in the class actually listened as we delivered our presentations.

One of the members of the class was a young woman from my high school whom I had admired from afar for some time. She was beautiful, graceful, and full of charm. I thought she was wonderful, and wondered why someone like her would be in a class on public speaking. She was the type of young woman who could cause a group to cease all conversation just by entering the room because every eye would be on her as she walked through!

As her time came to stand before the class to give her ten-minute speech, she walked to the front of the room, stood silently before the class for a few moments, began to quietly say a few words, and then she suddenly burst into tears and ran to her seat with her hands covering her face. I was stunned! Kathleen was afraid to speak before such a small audience! I initially felt sorry for her and even approached her to comfort her. But at the same time, I became filled with a feeling of comfort and a sense of empowerment that if she, whom I had admired for so long, was afraid to stand before that small audience and deliver her speech, then I knew that I could do it! She, through her response to her fear of presenting a speech in front of an audience, gave me the courage that in spite of my stuttering and fear of embarrassment, I could give my speech and do the best that I could! And I did! I stood before the class and gave my ten-minute speech without a hitch! To say the least, I was proud! And I even received a good grade for my presentation! I told Kathleen that if I could do it, she could do it too. And she did!

Travis Bradbury writes about the "10 Communication Secrets of Great Leaders," which could be altered nicely to "10 Communication Secrets of Great Presenters," along with Sarah Lloyd-Hughes who writes about the "Six Qualities of an Inspiring Speaker." Both authors reflect on similar but slightly different qualities of persons who are able to inspire and impact positively on others by their ability to communicate, including speaking before an audience of a few or thousands.

What makes a great presenter or a great communicator? Here are a few qualities as outlined by Bradbury:[2]

1. They know their audience.

Great communicators don't worry about sounding important, showing off their expertise, or boosting their own egos. They think about what people need or want to hear and how they can deliver the message so that people will be able to hear it (and understand it).

2. They are experts in body language.

Great communicators are constantly tracking people's reactions to what they are saying. They are quick to pick up on cues like facial expressions and body language because they know that that is the only feedback many people in the audience will give them. Great communicators use this feedback to tailor their message on the fly and adjust their communication style as needed.

3. They are authentic.

Great communicators don't try to be someone they are not just because they have stepped onto a stage and picked up a microphone. There's a reason Mark Zuckerberg presented his proposal for his concept called "Facebook" to investors wearing a hoodie and blue jeans. Great leaders know that when they stay true to who they are, people gravitate to their message.

4. They speak with authority.

Great communicators don't try to cover their backs by being ambiguous, wishy-washy, or unassertive.

Instead, they stick their necks out and speak directly about how things are and how they need to be.

5. They speak to groups as individuals.

In a nutshell, whether it's a huddle around a conference table or an overflowing auditorium, great leaders know how to work the room and make every person feel as if he or she is being spoken to directly.

And remember, according to Bradbury, no one ever became a great leader without first becoming a great communicator.

According to Lloyd-Hughes in her book *How to be Brilliant at Public Speaking*, there are six qualities of an inspiring speaker. As she says, "What is it that makes one public speaker inspiring and another just okay? Is it a list of rules, or something else?"[3]

According to her, everyone already has everything that is needed to become an inspiring speaker. Public speaking *rules* don't make an inspiring public speaker. Public speaking rules are saying, "Don't be yourself, be someone else." That doesn't make a great public speaker!

A great presenter is a speaker who uses her or his own set of natural qualities, their own natural abilities that make them appealing in their own way. They are their own person, not a speaker who is following a set a public speaking rules! Martin Luther King Jr. did not give his "I Have a Dream" speech by following a set of public speaking rules. He spoke from the heart, using his own natural qualities and his own sincerity to get his message across to that vast audience!

So what are six qualities of an inspiring presenter? Lloyd-Hughes gives us the following:

1. *Awareness*

Awareness is the quality that allows you *choice* over your actions as a speaker. Developing awareness allows you to pick up on the behaviors that serve your audience and drop the ones that distract the audience from your message.

2. *Empathy*

Most speakers start their speech preparation by asking themselves "What do I want to say?" But an inspiring speaker starts from the perspective of their audience, seeking primarily to serve *their*, the audience's, goals for attending the presentation. In doing so, the speaker becomes one who is listened to and respected.

3. *Freshness*

Freshness is the quality that gives *ZING* to any talk. Freshness allows a speaker to be unique, spontaneous, and memorable.

4. *Balance*

Balance refers to the ability to judge which information goes in and which stays out. That is, what is important that will take your audience on an incredible journey through your ability as a public speaker.

5. *Fearlessness*

Fearlessness refers to the ability to go beyond your comfort zone in service to your audience. This is the quality that brings edginess and power to any public speaker, so the audience can see just how important the topic is to you.

6. *Authenticity*

The final and perhaps most important quality is the ability to be yourself even if you feel rather vulnerable and even if it feels in some way inappropriate. Your authenticity connects to your audience's humanity and allows them to also be authentic. This is the quality that transforms public presentation from "technically good" to "Wow!"

Even if a speaker isn't 100 percent confident or doesn't catch 100 percent of traditionally "good" speaking technique, they can still inspire by developing these six qualities. "You can inspire by being yourself, rather than trying to be someone you are not."[4]

So how do we become a great presenter?

The Three P's

Remember, there are no "natural born" public speakers. We become a great public speaker with the three P's. Those are *practice* and *patience* and *perspiration!*

No one becomes a great presenter the first time in front of an audience. To assist myself in "correcting" my severe stuttering, I took it upon myself to enter every speaking opportunity I could find. I auditioned for parts in every play in high school and college, and I captured every opportunity I could find that provided an outlet for speaking either in club meetings or to public. The premise upon which I entered this arena of speaking in public was that I felt that if I experienced moments of success in speaking, those small successes might develop into bigger successes, and perhaps eventually I could develop into a fluent speaker. In other words, perhaps some success might breed further successes!

I was reluctantly allowed by my high school and college speech coaches to enter competitions in debate, extemporaneous speaking, and oratory. I was particularly good at extemporaneous speaking because when the competitor is given a topic she or he is then provided sixty seconds to develop the presentation, and the presentation begins without rehearsal. There is no time to become nervous or to fret about stuttering!

As I entered college, I continued to place myself in situations that required speaking. During my senior year, among those "places" that required speaking was intercollegiate oratory in which the competitors were to prepare and give twelve- to fifteen-minute competitive orations from memory. The day of the state men's oratory competition, I was to drive to one of the large universities in our state of Kansas, about 90 miles away from our farm. It was winter, and it was snowing. After arriving and walking through a grassy field of mud and snowy slush, I finally arrived at the correct building. But the lower one-third of the pants of the new blue suit and my new shoes were covered with mud.

I hurried to the room where the competition was being held, slowly opened the door, and found that there was still time to deliver my oration. I walked without hesitation to the front of the speaker's room, faced the judges and the other orators and their coaches who were seated near them, and without forethought began my 15-minute oration from memory. I was so concerned about being late and the appearance of mud on my shoes and the slacks, I did not have time to build any level of anxiety. If there were dysfluencies, I tried to use them as pauses for purposes of emphasis.

At the conclusion of my oration, I simply thanked the judges, walked from the room, and drove the 90 miles back to our farm in central Kansas. I was embarrassed by what I thought had been a poor performance. At about 9:00 P.M., the telephone rang and my mother answered. She said that my forensics coach wanted to speak with me. As I put the receiver to my ear, he was almost beside himself with excitement. He was informing me that I had won first place in the Kansas State Intercollegiate Men's Oratory Competition, the first time it had happened to anyone from our small college! It was difficult for me to believe what had just happened, that I was the best orator of the best from the colleges and universities in my state! It was a grand achievement in the life of a stutterer!

The Final Chapter

At that point, my stuttering extinguished to the degree that I was essentially fluent most of the time, and I have been since that time. Everything seemed to boil down to the fact that my original plan was the best one. *Success does breed success!* That has been and continues to be my premise. At this time in my adult life I am still a stutterer, but I am able to control it to the point that it is unnoticeable. Today, this former stutterer is a sought-after public speaker on, "The Art of Communication in Professional Practice," quite a turnabout from my many prior years of embarrassment as a severe stutterer.

So what does it take to become an accomplished public speaker? Practice, patience, and perspiration!

Practice

As I said above, it takes *practice, patience,* and *perspiration* to become an accomplished presenter! We must place ourselves in situations that provide opportunities for *practice.* Those include committee meetings, church organizations, moving on to community and state organizations. Once we polish our manner of presentation and our style of speaking, we can give ourselves a "brand" or a topic or subject matter that gives us our "brand," whether it be motivational, inspirational, or political. In other words, we must have a subject matter or topic that becomes attached to *us*, that we are invited to speak about at conferences and conventions. Perhaps you may even want to locate an agent who will locate venues for your presentations! And in your wildest dreams, you become a circuit speaker who travels around the country to give presentations as a result of the grand way you have developed as a public speaker!

Patience

Second of all, you must have *patience*. As I said earlier, there is no such thing as a natural-born public presenter. We may have seen speakers who possess what appears to be a natural outgoing personality and can speak in a confident and articulate manner. To be a dynamic public speaker, one must develop a number of traits that represent excellence in public speaking that are addressed in this book, and that takes both *practice* and *patience*.

Perspiration

Third, becoming a dynamic presenter requires a great deal of *perspiration!* That's where *practice* and *patience* comes in. If you think back on my story that describes the years in which I practiced speaking and the situations in which I placed myself to become an accomplished public speaker, you have an inkling of what is required. Of course, not all of you are diagnosed as stutterers. But to become one who possesses all the requirements of an accomplished public speaker that are presented in this book, some amount of *perspiration* is ultimately required!

So *practice*, have *patience*, and *perspire* a little as you place yourself in situations that require presenting before an audience. You will be amazed at how your finesse as an accomplished platform speaker will develop. You will be great!

Notes

1. Chad Schultz, "Do People Really Fear Public Speaking More Than Death?" TM Vision, June 25, 2011, http://tmvision.org/speaking/people-fear-public-speaking-death.

2. Andrew Bradbury, *Successful Presentation Skills* (London: Kogan Page, 2010).

3   Sarah Lloyd-Hughes, *How to Be Brilliant at Public Speaking: Any Audience, Any Situation* (Harlow, England: Prentice Hall Life/Pearson, 2011).

4. Ibid.

CHAPTER TWO

THE POWER OF PRESENTATION

By Jim Stovall

It's easy to believe that we live in a world of solid objects, concrete boundaries, and absolute facts. In reality, our world is filled with thoughts, ideas, and concepts that are brought to us from the minds of other people. The way that these thoughts, ideas, and concepts come to us is through a complex vehicle we will call a presentation.

We often think of presentations as someone telling us what happened in the past or communicating the current state of affairs, but in reality presentations have changed the world we live in and altered history.

Victor Hugo is known for saying, "Nothing is more powerful than an idea whose time has come." An idea only becomes powerful when it can be shared with others in the form of a presentation.

I have long been fascinated by communicating with others through a variety of presentation methods. Today, as a professional speaker, I have the privilege of making presentations to literally millions of people, but I also run an international television network; have authored over 30 books, six of which have been turned into movies; write a weekly syndicated column; and do a weekly national radio program. Each of these methods of communicating are simply different ways to make a presentation.

One of my movie partners may have said it best when he stated, "When you can tell a great story, you earn the right to communicate your message." In our world of instant communication, many people are confusing contacting someone with truly communicating with other people. Just because you have a message doesn't make it relevant, and just because you've delivered your message doesn't mean you've communicated. And even if you've communicated, it doesn't mean your audience has received the message you intended.

Your presentation is the only conduit between you and your audience. It's much like a broadcast in that it can be delayed, distorted, corrupted, or even canceled, leaving your audience with a faulty presentation or no presentation at all. The only thing that may be worse than not communicating is to assume you have communicated when you truly have not delivered your message.

Over 20 years ago, I discovered an amazing career generically known as professional speaking. I believe we're all put here on earth for a reason, and I discovered a major part of my reason for being here the first time I walked onto a stage to make a speech. It felt like putting my foot into my shoe. It just fit. I found that I could deliver humor, deep emotion, and powerful information that could influence my audience far into the future.

At the highest level, professional speakers are extremely well compensated. After a number of years of struggling to the top of the profession, I found myself being paid as much for a one-hour speech as the average family in my state receives in annual income. Partially as a result of this windfall, I made a commitment to do one speech for free for each one for which I am paid. These *pro bono* speeches are generally made to nonprofit organizations and schools in my hometown and surrounding area.

During one of these unpaid speeches, I met an unforgettable individual named Reverend Charles Neal. Reverend Neal had been the head of a local congregation and nonprofit organization in my hometown for many years. At the time we met, he was in his late 80s and was one of the most vibrant and vigorous individuals I ever met. As we were introducing ourselves to one another, I couldn't help but notice he had a very pronounced and compelling British accent. When I asked him about it, he told me he had grown up in England and had not moved to America until after World War II.

As our conversation continued, I realized that Reverend Neal was one of the most well-read, well-traveled, and most interesting people I had ever met. After the day of my speech, we stayed in touch and exchanged thoughts, ideas, and a number of recommended book titles.

I clearly remember the day I was talking with Reverend Neal about the greatest public speakers of all time. I had been collecting audio recordings of the best speakers and presenters throughout history. I shared with Reverend Neal my enthusiasm for the speeches and presentation style of Winston Churchill, and I told him, "Winston Churchill was one of the best speakers I have ever heard."

That was when Reverend Neal pulled back the curtain and revealed a significant part of his earlier life when he told me that he had worked for Churchill during the war and for several years after World War II. The plot thickened when he told me he had worked for Churchill as a speechwriter and had actually written Churchill's famous Iron Curtain speech.

There are times in life when you find yourself communicating with someone as an equal or a peer when you discover that they are a world-class talent within the area of your discussion.

Reverend Neal was very kind and continued to treat me as an equal and one of his contemporaries in the speaking arena. Then he asked a question that powerfully influenced my perspective on the realm of presentation. He remarked, "You mentioned Churchill was one of the best speakers you have ever heard. Who do you believe was the best?" This created a potentially awkward situation as I had not known of Reverend Neal's relationship to Churchill when I had made the statement, but believing that honesty is always the best policy, I told him candidly that I thought Adolf Hitler was the best speaker I had ever heard.

Reverend Neal chuckled and then began to laugh uproariously. Fearing I had said something inappropriate or even embarrassing, I asked, "Did I say something wrong?" Reverend Neal patted my shoulder and said, "No, young man, you did not say anything inappropriate. In fact, your admiration of Mr. Hitler's speaking ability was shared by Mr. Churchill."

He told me that Winston Churchill had believed that the outcome of the war depended greatly upon the speeches and radio broadcasts he made himself contrasted with those speeches and radio broadcasts made by Adolf Hitler.

This launched a number of conversations between me and Reverend Neal about Churchill and Hitler. For the first time, I began to understand the difference between a presentation and a message. Adolf Hitler arguably had the most disgusting, depraved, and morally bankrupt messages in history, but his presentations were so powerful that he came frighteningly close to taking over the world.

When I began to understand this concept fully, I realized that anyone with a powerful message has a responsibility to give that message the quality of presentation that it deserves. A pure, positive, and powerful message with a faulty presentation will fail to deliver the impact and fall far short of the message's potential.

According to Reverend Neal, Churchill believed and often said, "We will live in a free world as long as Franklin Roosevelt can speak into a microphone." President Roosevelt was very ill and infirmed but was able to deliver a powerful and positive message to all Americans and the allies around the world via his radio presentations.

As a blind person myself, I have often thought that it was a tremendous benefit to the war effort and the cause of freedom that Franklin Roosevelt could not be seen in his wheelchair, but instead, his message was delivered through his powerful and confident voice to people around the world.

Even though I am blind, I remain constantly aware of the fact that my audience is not. The way I appear and move impacts my message. Ironically, when I first began speaking, my audiences were understandably small. Then, over time, I was hired to speak to larger and larger groups. Through this progression, I became aware of the fact that my gestures and movements needed to get larger and grander if they were going to have an impact on the entire audience.

Then I remember the first time I spoke at an arena event with an IMAG setup. This involves a multi-camera production that projects the speaker's image onto giant screens throughout the arena. I found myself instantly in a situation where I had to make my presentation as if I were back speaking to small audiences again, because the majority of the people in the arena were watching me on a movie screen and could readily and easily observe every minor expression and gesture.

You can't communicate your message without being mindful of your presentation, and you can't be mindful of your presentation without being aware of the audience's perspective. It is often helpful to separate the presentation from the message to understand the validity and power of each.

I'm a huge fan of satellite radio, which can bring dozens of talk shows to me at any given time. Some of these programs are presented from a perspective with which I agree, and other programs are presented from a perspective that I do not agree with either politically or philosophically, but this often makes it easier to evaluate the presentation.

Just as Hitler could make a great and powerful presentation with a horrible message, there are countless people who are suffering a lack of success because they are poorly presenting what otherwise could be a powerful message.

In addition to the diverse talk shows, satellite radio has brought me total access to my beloved St. Louis Cardinals throughout the baseball season. Being able to listen to the Cardinals' broadcaster presenting the game and then switching over to listen to the other team's broadcaster has helped me to develop an interesting perspective on presentations. You can have two veteran broadcasters each observing the same game at the same time, but they have virtually opposite presentations. What may be a "great play and tremendous effort" in the presentation of the Cardinals' broadcaster may be "a poor effort and disappointing result" in the words of the opposition's broadcaster.

Presentation is always a product of perspective. We always have a bias, and the most honest and objective way to deal with our bias is to reveal it up front as a part of the presentation.

In every generation, there are presentations and presenters that change the culture and alter history. My parents and grandparents are a product of Franklin Roosevelt's statements such as, "We have nothing to fear but fear itself," and Winston Churchill's admonitions including, "Let them say that this was our finest hour." In my generation, I remember President Kennedy's advice, "Ask not what your country can do for you. Ask what you can do for your country," as well as Martin Luther King's presentation for the ages which communicated, "I have a dream."

One need not technically be a great presenter in order to make a great presentation if they have power and passion behind their message. I have received many awards and honors in my career. They are humbling and an attribute to my colleagues who have dedicated themselves to our message and the presentations we make. I am very proud to have been recognized as the International Humanitarian of the Year. Previous recipients of this honor included Jimmy Carter, Nancy Reagan, and Mother Teresa.

Mother Teresa had won the award prior to the year they were recognizing me, so I did some research so I could honor her appropriately in my own acceptance speech. Among the many inspiring and life-affirming stories I heard and read about Mother Teresa was one about a particular presentation she made. As the story was related to me, Mother Teresa was called upon to give a speech to a number of affluent New Yorkers at the Waldorf Astoria Hotel. Mother Teresa had been working constantly for months in India with orphans who lived under the most difficult and impoverished conditions imaginable. Coming from that realm of disease and hunger into the opulence of the ballroom and being confronted by an affluent and somewhat arrogant audience, Mother Teresa decided to alter her planned presentation. She had been scheduled to speak for a full hour after the sumptuous dinner, but as she was introduced, Mother Teresa walked to the podium and delivered a poignant presentation that took only a couple of minutes. She looked over that vast audience of privileged patrons and stated, "Last month in my country, one thousand children died because they didn't have enough food to eat; and this month in my country, another one thousand children are dying because they don't have enough food to eat; and I fear that next month in my country still another one thousand children will die because they don't have enough food to eat. And as I look out over this audience after the wonderful meal you have consumed, I am struck by the fact that you don't give a damn."

Mother Teresa paused at that point in the presentation to allow her audience to react to her words, and then she concluded by saying, "And the worst thing is that most of you are more concerned by my use of a four-letter word than the lives of three thousand children."

Mother Teresa left the podium and walked off the stage as the audience sat in stunned silence. Those who had expected an hour-long presentation of hope to be delivered by one of the world's best-known humanitarians may have been disappointed. Technically, her presentation may not have been a success, but when you understand that a record-breaking amount of money was raised that night, resulting in many sick children being treated and fed, you would have to conclude Mother Teresa gave both a powerful and a successful presentation.

The success of a presentation can only be measured against the presentation's purpose. A presentation can teach, inform, inspire, or entertain. The most entertaining academic lecture that did not deliver the lesson could never be considered a success; the most humorous motivational presentation that failed to inspire did not meet its goal; and the most technically correct presentation that was intended to entertain but left the audience unfulfilled could not be considered worth the time and effort that the presentation required. Presentations have changed the world in which we live. Presentations have impacted every area of our lives.

The very best and the very worst presentations are both impactful. It's easy to observe the power and impact of a great presentation, while the results of a poor presentation in the form of negative impact and wasted potential are not so readily apparent.

Delivering a presentation is not just a job or a task to be fulfilled. It is a responsibility that carries consequences far beyond the presentation. We are all a product of the presentations that have been made to us in the past, and we influence those around us on a regular basis through the presentations we make.

CHAPTER THREE

The Art of Preparing Your Presentation: How Do I Know If What I Am Preparing Is What My Audience Wants to Hear?

By Ray Hull, PhD

Preparing a presentation is one of the most difficult aspects of public presentations. What do I say? How do I inspire the audience to actually listen to me? What if they find me to be a complete bore? What if I look at the audience after ten minutes into my speech and they are already falling asleep? What if I don't say anything important?

Well, asking all of those questions is what most public speakers do while developing their presentation. It is a natural anticipatory response to wondering how an audience will respond to what we say when we are standing on stage before them with a microphone in our hand waiting to utter the first words of our presentation. As I said in Chapter One, we tend to feel vulnerable when we are standing before an audience. We wonder whether what we are going to say to them will interest them or bore them!

There have been occasions in my professional life when I have given the same presentation twenty-five times. As I am preparing to give it each time, I revise and revise again. That's right! When I have prepared that same speech for the twenty-sixth time and am still revising it, I am doing it for a reason. Each time I present that speech, I watch the audience. There always seem to be times when they appear to be very attentive. They appear to be holding on to every word. And then there may be times during the presentation when they may appear almost disinterested in what I am saying. I make mental notes of those moments. And, if I feel that what I am saying at those points in the presentation is critical to what I am intending to say, then I must be doing something wrong in how I am presenting it. So I study it, make slight changes in the words I have chosen and how I am delivering the information. Then present it the next time with those adjustments in mind. If the audience appears interested and attentive the next time I reach that critical point in the presentation, then I know that perhaps what I am doing at that critical point is more effective than what I was doing before.

How Do I Prepare a Speech So That I Know I Am Doing It Correctly?

Okay, let's say that you have been asked by a local organization to give a presentation on a project that you have been working on that will enhance the beauty of the community in which you and those who will be in attendance at the meeting live. The intent of your presentation is to raise the funds that will support the project. What you say and how you say it may make or break the fund-raising effort. How you prepare your presentation will, of course, determine its content, and you are hoping that the content will convince those in the audience to help finance the upgrade project for the community in which you all live.

Piece of cake, right? If everyone loves their community, then all you will need to say is "Give us money and we'll do great things for you." Wrong! Money is tight, and people must be convinced beyond a doubt that their money will be well spent and the project will do what it is supposed to do—that is, to beautify the community at a reasonable cost.

So, how do I prepare the presentation? Steve Brown[1] says it this way. He states that the first item on your preparatory agenda is to:

Consider the Audience

We have to consider the hard, cold fact that it is the audience who determines whether a speech is good or poor. It is the audience who determines whether what you have said is worthwhile or a waste of time. When we consider the audience, we need to take into account several things, such as:

a. What is the average age and gender of the audience?

b. What is the average educational level of the audience?

c. Will the audience be hostile, supportive, or neutral?

d. What is the attention span of the audience?

e. In the past, has the audience responded positively or negatively to presentations in which financial support has been requested?

Those are all fair questions to ask yourself prior to developing your presentation. In other words, your knowledge of the audience will dictate the content and style of your speech. If you don't take the audience into consideration, your presentation may be great in and of itself, but it won't do what you wanted it to do—to be a great fundraiser and to raise money for the community project.

When you develop your presentation that has as its purpose raising funds for the beautification project, you will know that money is tight, the economy is tight. Everyone will be aware of that fact. So, why not begin your presentation with something like, *"I am well aware that money is tight. My own budget is tight! But I also know that we love our community, and we want to make it a place that we are all proud of. So I know that together, we can all contribute a little to make a big difference!"*

You are speaking in simple terms, you are speaking from the heart, and you are not pretending to be someone else. You are believable.

President Clinton won his first election primarily by identifying a big need in the U.S., the U.S. economy, and then applying logic that would solve it. In his campaign headquarters, he had a banner that read, *"Keep It Simple!"* And it worked! That is what he used to win his first term as President. He spoke in simple terms that everyone could understand. And that is your job in making a presentation that will raise funds for your community beautification project.

Questions to Ask Yourself When Designing Your Presentation

According to Toogood,[2] there are questions that a presenter needs to ask her or himself when developing a presentation. Those are:

1. Why is what I am saying important?

2. If not, what should I really be saying?

3. What is the point of what I am saying?

4. Am I speaking in a language everyone can understand?

5. Who really cares?

Essential Elements of a Good Presentation

What are the essential elements of a good presentation that we should know before we prepare it? I don't suppose I should use the word *good* here, but rather a *great* presentation! To me, *good* refers to *average*. You want your presentation to be a great one rather than an average one!

Toogood refers to five key elements that should be kept in mind as you develop your presentation. Those are:

1. A Strong Start

Make your first statement a dramatic one! Not necessarily loud, but dramatic. Our voice carries the drama of our part in any play or in any presentation. As I said earlier, your first statement in your fundraising presentation could be, in a somewhat strong but empathetic voice, something like, "I know that money is tight. It's tight in my household too! But our community is important to us, and together we can make it one that we can all be proud of. *We can all give a little to make a big difference!*"

Wow! I like that first statement! It is not a dramatic one, but it is a strong one! That is the key to a good introductory statement. It needs to be one that will draw the attention of the audience.

2. One Theme, One Topic

One topic. Stick to a single topic, and make it brief.

3. Use Good Examples

Using good examples to strengthen the logic of your presentation gives it the boost that will make what you are saying stick with the audience.

4. Use Conversational Language

That's what made President Clinton and President Obama stand out as leaders. President Bush had difficulty choosing words, even pronouncing them correctly, and was ridiculed for that as a result. Keep your language simple and to the point. Use language that everyone will understand, speak slowly enough to be easily understood, and you will be considered an excellent public speaker. The best advice is to simply talk to your audience as you would a friend!

5. Give a Strong Ending

A key phrase that you develop can be used to make a strong ending. For example, in point one above, the key phrase for the beginning that was used as an example could also be used for a strong ending, *"We can all give a little to make a big difference! I know we can!"* A simple phrase said with passion that people will remember can give your presentation the strength to make an impression on your audience. It will give them something that they will remember!

Be a Creative Speech Maker

When developing your presentation, be creative. The problem is, as we become mature adults we tend to become less creative. The most creative beings are young children. Their minds are open to new and creative ideas. They are creative and playful. As adults, we tend to fear making mistakes. As Thomas Edison once said, paraphrased, "I didn't make a mistake, I just found one more of 10,000 ways that don't work!" He had a creative mind, and that is one of many reasons he was a great inventor. If we are going to become a great speech maker, we have to be creative. Giving presentations in a creative way will cause our presentations to be remembered.

According to Reynolds in his book *Presentation Zen*, there are three ways in which we can bring about our creative self that can be used when we are developing our presentations.[3] They are:

1. Be Creative—Be a Pirate!

Inspiration is important! Reynolds asks, "Where can you find inspiration?" Probably not by doing the same old routine or by gossiping with staff in the break room about things that really don't matter. Reynolds says, "The enthusiasm of a student is infectious and can energize you. Be careless, be reckless! Be a lion! Be a pirate! You know it's important to be free, free like children. You just need to be reminded of that occasionally."

2. Don't Force It

Idling or doing nothing is important. Most of us, as Reynolds says (myself included), are obsessed with getting things done. We're afraid to be unproductive. And yet the big ideas often come to us during our periods of "laziness." People need more time away from the direct challenges of work. Sometimes we need solitude and a break for slowing down so that we can see things differently.

3. Enthusiasm

Reynolds further stresses, "Put your love, passion, imagination, and spirit behind what you are developing! Without enthusiasm, there is no creativity. ...Don't hang out with people who dismiss the idea of enthusiasm. Or worse still, don't hang out with those who try to kill yours."

A Final Word on Developing Your Presentation

A final word on preparing your presentation is important here. It is imperative that we take into consideration the following items, not only in regard to preparing your presentation, but also in preparing how you will say what you intend to say. Print them indelibly in your mind. They are:

1. Your presentation should be relevant to the intent of that specific occasion.

2. Your presentation should be simple.

3. It should be to the point and as brief as possible. If you are given 30 minutes for your presentation and you take 20 minutes, the audience will be pleased. If you are given 30 minutes and you take 45 minutes, don't be surprised to see members of your audience beginning to squirm, wishing that you would stop.

4. Once you have prepared your speech, cut it, cut it, cut it.[4] You will be surprised how

lengthy a speech can become after it is written word-for-word. A speech written word-for-word will almost always be considerably longer than you expect it to be if you allow yourself to read it to the audience. On the other hand, *never* read your speech to your audience! If you do, expect to see a sizeable number dozing off after the first fifteen minutes.

5. There are questions we should ask ourselves before beginning the preparation of a public presentation. Hindle[5] suggests that we ask following questions:

- What is the expected size of the audience?

- What is the average age of the audience? It is very important to know the average age of the audience to whom you will be speaking, particularly in regard to the language level you will be using.

- Is the audience already well informed about your subject matter?

- Has the audience been required to attend, or are they there on a voluntary basis?

- What do the members of the audience have in common? Are they all from the same academic or occupational field, the same demographic area, with the same interests, and with the same reason for being in attendance?

- Are there prejudices that the audience may hold that need to be considered in preparing your speech?

- What is the cultural makeup of the audience?

- Does everyone in the audience know you or at least know you by reputation?

Be Sure to Ask Even More Questions

Prior to preparing your presentation, and importantly before you make your presentation, ask more questions of those who invited you to speak.

1. Ask about the physical space where you will be speaking.

2. Ask about the makeup of the audience. Otherwise you may be surprised or even embarrassed as you begin making your presentation.

I have found myself speaking at a convention on stage in a large auditorium that could hold 500 people when there were only 11 people in the audience. I came prepared with around 200 handouts, my Power Point slides, and required an excellent PA system and hand-held microphone (I don't like to stand behind a podium). I could have avoided the stage and the PA system, moved down on the floor level, and asked those in attendance to move closer to me so we could talk. We could have had a nice, intimate conversation instead of a formal stage presentation! This occurred because I forgot to ask about the potential size of the audience!

I have also given presentations at conventions on stage in a large auditorium that could hold over 850 people when there was standing room only in the back of the auditorium, chairs filled with people in each of the aisles, and even one attendee sitting on stage with me! I didn't have enough handouts, but the stage, spotlight, PA system, and Power Point slides were perfect, and about 1,000 people filled every nook and cranny of the auditorium!

The problem that I experienced was that I did not ask questions ahead of time. And if we don't ask questions, we will never know how things will turn out until we walk onto the stage!

Notes

1. Stephen W. Brown, *How to Talk so People Will Listen* (Grand Rapids, MI: Baker Book House, 1999).

2. Granville N. Toogood, *The Articulate Executive* (New York: McGraw-Hill, 1996).

3. Garr Reynolds, Presentation Zen: Simple Ideas on Presentation Design and Delivery (Berkeley, CA: New Riders Pub., 2008).

4. Tim Hindle, *Making Presentations* (New York: DK Pub., 1998).

5. Ibid.

CHAPTER FOUR

OUR PAST PRESENTATIONS

By Jim Stovall

We are all products of the presentations we have made as well as the presentations that have been made to us in our past. To a great extent, we succeed or fail based on our ability to make powerful and impactful presentations. Our presenting skills or lack thereof come greatly from our past and presentations that have been made to us.

Our earliest presentations often come to us from our parents, other family members, or friends who surrounded us when we were young children. My earliest memories of presentations were those given to me by my parents and grandparents. Many of those powerful messages remain with me today. "If you're not ten minutes early, you're late," "Be the best at whatever you choose to do," and "Always do what you said you would do," are among the earliest messages that came to me from presentations that still impact me to this day.

It is easy to take for granted the powerful positive messages we have received through presentations early in our lives until we encounter other people who faced verbal abuse and negative messages through presentations early in their lives. A powerful presentation is impactful whether it's the history-changing speech from Martin Luther King or the evil messages delivered in presentations from Adolf Hitler.

As healthy, achieving, successful people, we have to constantly filter presentations that are made to us in the present day and re-filter and re-label negative presentations that were made to us in the past.

I have met people whose earliest memories of presentations were from abusive, misguided parents or other caretakers who told them, "You are stupid, ugly, and will never amount to anything." These impactful statements have to undergo reevaluation and reprogramming if those people are going to reach their full potential. We must always be mindful of the fact that our words and presentations have an impact, particularly on young children who are very impressionable.

As an adult, if someone approaches me today and declares, "You are stupid, ugly, and will never amount to anything," I have evidence I can use to reason through, evaluate, and dismiss their comments; but these words delivered to a child in a presentation can be disastrous as they often have no experience or worldview that can allow them to diminish or dismiss a harmful message. I am blessed to have been impacted by many powerful messages from great presenters throughout my formative years.

Recently, I was watching the Grammy Award show. It was fascinating to hear the acceptance speeches by the world's greatest musical artists. I was struck by the fact that many of them credited their earliest musical influences to singing or hearing music sung in a church. Many of us experienced our earliest formal presentations in a church service. Whether the service was inspiring, exhilarating, or boring, it's likely those memories remain with us to this day and influence how we feel about church services.

I remember sitting in a church service and having my first thoughts of being a public speaker myself. When I was 10 or 11 years old, my parents joined a new church. It was one of the huge downtown congregations whose service was televised each week. Possibly because my younger brother and I could have tended to be a bit noisy and disruptive, my parents chose to sit in the balcony along the side of the sanctuary. My seat became the last seat in the row so I was looking at the profile of the minister as he stood at the podium to speak.

From this vantage point, I could watch the minister speak to the congregation, and I could experience their reactions. I could see the notes he had on the podium in front of him and could observe the timeclock and the red and green TV lights that he used to make sure he finished his message on time.

My pastor for the next four or five years was one of the most gifted presenters I have ever heard. I was struck by the fact that he was speaking to a group of people live and delivering a message to a television as well as a radio audience at the same time. Delivering presentations to these various audiences required different skill sets and methods, but somehow—week after week—he was able to impactfully communicate with each of the audiences.

I found myself visiting the church's library every Sunday morning before the service because I knew the pastor would be in there going over his notes or checking a few last-minute references before his Sunday morning message. We struck up a regular weekly dialogue about his previous week's message as well as the one he was planning later that same morning. Without my knowing it, this constituted my early education in public speaking and the art of presentation.

We remained good friends even after he retired, and I called on him many times to discuss various speeches or his thoughts on how best to present a concept.

He passed away several years later, but I remain a product of his presenting skills and his willingness to mentor a boy, a young man, and eventually a professional speaker.

Virtually all of us were positively or negatively impacted by presentations made in school. It is likely that we formed our impressions of, and preference for, history, math, literature, and many other fields of study from our earliest days in school and the way those subjects were presented to us.

Because of the success of my novel *The Ultimate Gift* and the movie based on it along with the sequel books and movies, I have the privilege of speaking at many schools both in person and via satellite. Through this process, I have met many teachers and countless students. I am amazed that some teachers can make any topic tedious or boring while other teachers create magic, mystery, and excitement around the same topic.

I have been in history classes where they were studying World War II. I have heard teachers droning on, *ad nauseam*, as bored and distracted students struggled to stay awake. Throughout recorded history, there are few chapters of human endeavor that have ever offered as much excitement, power, and passion as the study of World War II. Countless books, movies, and television programs continue to document the colorful and world-changing war years.

I am baffled as to how a teacher of history can present World War II in a way that it becomes boring. I have been in English literature classrooms where hormonally-charged teenagers are being lectured about Romeo and Juliet, but the presentation is so convoluted and watered down that the passion of Shakespeare's message is lost in the impotent presentation.

On the other hand, there are teachers of literature who continue to light the fires of passion in their students for the written word. These teachers take the same material that some of their weaker colleagues have access to, but they masterfully present their subject in such a way that their presentations resonate for decades after their students have graduated.

For more than 20 years at this writing, I have written a weekly syndicated column read by millions of people around the world via newspapers, magazines, and online publications; and, as many of my 30 previous books have become international bestsellers, I remain acutely aware that many, if not most, of my readers live outside the United States. We Americans must always remember that our presentations may be local in scope but international in impact. In an ever-increasing way, our audiences are from different countries, cultures, and backgrounds.

Here in America, our leaders are selected through a somewhat complex and convoluted political process. Politicians are elected by running successful campaigns. A campaign is nothing, more or less, than a presentation that goes on for many months. While there are countless hours of speeches and endless sound bites, political careers have been made or lost on the turn of one impactful phrase that sticks in the minds and consciousness of the public.

Political historians can point to the very speeches that gave rise to the political careers of such world leaders as John F. Kennedy, Ronald Reagan, or Bill Clinton. On the other hand, a single poor political presentation can arguably account for the downfall of the public careers of Vice President Dan Quayle, Governor Rick Perry, Senator Howard Dean, and many others.

My late, great friend and mentor legendary coach John Wooden was fond of telling his players, "You will be known for a lifetime of good deeds or one momentary lapse of judgement." This is true in life and the realm of presenting.

The days of saying something good or bad and having it fade into memory are gone. With the rise of digital technology, everything we say and do—especially our formal presentations—are a part of an ongoing irrevocable historical record. We know more about the world around us than any previous generation. The media bombards us with presentations, but we must be careful to filter each of these presentations for accuracy, bias, and perspective.

My late, great friend and mentor Paul Harvey became among the most influential figures of several generations as he delivered a daily presentation via his radio broadcast known as *Paul Harvey News and Comment*. I came to know Paul Harvey later as an author and professional speaker. He was as influential in those arenas as he was in the field of newscasting. Mr. Harvey always stressed to me and many others the importance of separating news from commentary.

In the presentations that many of us make, we deliver facts then offer opinions or conclusions. Opinions and conclusions are valid parts of a presentation, but they must be properly labeled. Too many presentations come to us delivering opinions labeled as facts. We must always respect our audience and anyone to whom we present enough to differentiate between our opinions and the absolute facts.

Before Paul Harvey impacted the world with his news and commentary, an entertaining cowboy from my home state of Oklahoma named Will Rogers touched the whole world with his wit and wisdom. Will Rogers was able to tackle some of the most difficult topics of the day in his radio broadcasts and daily columns using sarcasm and humor. Any great presentation will have some serious, poignant, emotional moments punctuated by humor.

Humor is not just an entertaining interlude but is an irreplaceable tool of a powerful presentation. Too many emotional moments piled upon one another will leave your audience drained. A brief laugh or comical anecdote can refresh your audience's palate for the next flavorful part of your presentation.

As Will Rogers taught us, the line between the facts, the fantasy, and the humor can be blurred in several ways. A presentation can be received by many people in many ways on many levels.

I am pleased that, at this writing, seven of my books have been turned into major motion pictures. In a movie, the story I created in my book is reworked to make an entirely new presentation utilizing the same message. I am pleased that in each of the films based on my novels, the audiences range from kindergartners to great-grandparents. The plots, topics, and subject matters remain relevant and interesting to everyone. This is a tribute to some very talented colleagues who have collaborated with me on these movie projects.

Any presentation needs to be tailored to the audience. A kindergarten teacher or the chief justice of the Supreme Court can each make a presentation about truth and honesty, but it will be structured in different ways to reach their individual audiences.

All of us have had the experience of receiving a message in a powerful presentation then reflecting upon past presentations that can now be viewed in a different light. The wisdom that tells us *when the pupil is ready, the teacher arrives* is a product of powerful presentations.

I have had great mentors throughout my life and career. Many of them have shared impactful messages with me that seemed complete in the moment, but years later with the benefit of experiences and hindsight those messages from my mentors can take on an even deeper meaning.

We have all reread a book or watched a movie multiple times and found new meaning that we somehow overlooked on previous occasions. A great presentation stays with the audience and can broaden and deepen as the audience's perspective grows and enables them to connect with more of the message than they could internalize initially.

I have had the distinct privilege of knowing several of the great speakers and presenters of our generation. I first knew them as a part of their audience through reading their books or listening to their speeches. Then, years later, I had the honor of sharing the stage with many of these luminaries.

I have always considered my late, great friend, mentor, and colleague Zig Ziglar as the dean of public speakers. Backstage at many of the huge arena events, speakers who are waiting their turn onstage are often found reviewing their notes, talking on the phone, or chatting with one another, but when Zig took the stage all the other speakers could be found standing in the wings watching the master work. Many of us could repeat Zig's stories word for word. They became such a part of our industry and our lives.

Zig Ziglar had a way of talking *with* his audience instead of talking *to* them or *at* them. He seemed to somehow ask them to consider what he was looking at as he observed the life around us and the possibilities for the future. Zig's stories created visual images as powerful as great movies.

Our culture has been shaped by the images from impactful motion pictures. A brief mention of film titles such as *Rocky, On Golden Pond, Caddyshack, ET,* or *Star Wars* will elicit verbatim lines of dialogue from those movies experienced decades ago. Great presenters and presentations create visual images and mental sound bites that endure.

Readers who have enjoyed any of my books, including this one, owe a debt of gratitude to Dr. Denis Waitley as much or more than to me. Like millions of people around the world, I became familiar with Dr. Denis Waitley through his book and presentation entitled *The Psychology of Winning.*

Denis came into my life at a time when I was losing my sight and learning to deal with the world as a blind person. I, as the pupil, was ready at the point when Denis Waitley, the teacher, arrived. There was a memorable point in each of Denis Waitley's presentations when he recited his poem entitled "If You Think You Can, You Can." Those words stayed with me and countless people among Denis's myriad of audience members throughout the years.

As a new fledgling speaker myself on tour with Denis and the legendary Dr. Robert Schuller, I was confronted by both of those giants about writing a book. This was something that had never crossed my mind, but great presenters introduce great possibilities, and before I knew it I had written my first book. Denis Waitley wrote the foreword to my initial book entitled *You Don't Have To Be Blind To See,* and Dr. Schuller opened the door with his publisher Thomas Nelson, which brought that project to life.

Thirty years after that initial encounter with Denis Waitley, he attended one of my speeches. The promotors of the event had alerted me that Dr. Waitley was in the audience, but he had asked if he could simply sit and watch and stay out of the limelight. This was simply not possible for me to do as I was standing on a stage that he had made a reality in my life.

I knew that evening that he had just celebrated his eightieth birthday, and I called him to the stage so I could pay tribute to him. Without thinking it through, I asked him in front of the entire audience if he could present his epic poem "If You Think You Can, You Can." It suddenly dawned on me that Dr. Waitley had not included that poem in his presentation for many years, but as any world-class presenter would do, Dr. Waitley recited that impactful poem word for word and indelibly influenced my audience and a whole new generation of people with the power of his presentation.

Think about all the great presentations that have impacted you throughout your life. Review the messages that you took away from those presentations, and consider what valuable wisdom may still be waiting for your enlightened mind to grasp. Great presentations are crafted for a lifetime not simply for the point of the presentation. Great words, messages, thoughts, ideas, and concepts resonate throughout history and are simply waiting to be rediscovered and reflected upon from a new angle of perspective.

Whether you're crafting a presentation or reviewing one, realize that the wisdom lies beneath the layers of the proverbial onion that you can peel back in days and years to come. When we fully understand this ongoing power of presentation, we become more diligent about the way we experience the presentation and the way we deliver a presentation.

CHAPTER FIVE

THE ART OF PRESENTATION

By Ray Hull, PhD

As I said in Chapter One, you are the artist. The stage or meeting room is your canvas. What you do with it is up to you. You can "wow" your audience by creating a masterpiece, or you can put them to sleep. Which do you choose? Of course you want to create a masterpiece and "wow" your audience! Why wouldn't you? But sometimes I find people who would rather hide behind the podium for the duration of their presentation and then at the conclusion attempt to creep off of the stage unseen. Hopefully that's not you.

It Isn't Necessary to Create a Masterpiece

It isn't always necessary to try to create a masterpiece. But we can create something that is acceptable, something that is good, and something that is liked and enjoyed. It doesn't have to be perfect to "wow" the audience. But it does need to be good.

I have given well over 800 presentations at conferences and conventions over the past 20 years. That's nearly two or more a month on the average. Occasionally, I am asked to give three or four presentations over a two-day period. The most I have been asked to give involved three different one-hour presentations in a consecutive three-hour period. I have done that several times, and by the third presentation I must admit that I have to do my best to bring myself up to my full capacity and say with enthusiastic feeling, "It is *great* to be here!" And mean it!

Being an Actor or Actress Helps!

To be a sought-after public speaker, an important addition to our repertoire of skills includes having some actor or actress within us. I tell my audiences that it is important to have a little bit of Fred Astaire the wonderful dancer and actor, the great French actor Maurice Chevalier, and a touch of Marcel Marceau the great French mime! That's a great deal to ask, but it takes at least a little of that to become a great public speaker!

To prepare myself to be the best public speaker I could possibly be, beside the fact that I was a severe stutterer from early childhood into adulthood, I auditioned for every play I could find and was asked to join the casts of plays with greater and greater frequency as the months and years passed. I made it into the casts of murder mysteries, musical comedy, Shakespearian plays, and a number of humorous and dramatic theatrical shows. I even made it into dinner theater, which I really didn't enjoy because rehearsals generally began at 10:00 PM after the performances were over for the evening.

I took tap dancing and auditioned to be a member of a dance team that engaged in stage dance and jazz ballet. I sang in musical comedy on stage, sang solos for talent shows, sang in madrigal groups for musical competitions, formed a gospel quartet that was popular (and still is!), and sang solos in stage shows.

When I was in high school and early college, I requested and was granted the opportunity by a local radio station to host my own radio show and was a rock and roll disk jockey for five years. I also did news broadcasts and commercials during and after I went off the air from my show.

This list could go on! What I am trying to say here is that in order to prepare yourself to be better than a "good" speaker, it is important to prepare yourself to feel comfortable in front of an audience.

Bad Experiences Can Help Us Too!

One of the worst experiences in which I found myself while trying to prepare myself to feel comfortable in front of an audience was while I was in high school. I auditioned to be the lead in a one-act play—a murder mystery that required the lead actor to straddle a chair that was turned around with the back of the chair toward the audience. With arms folded over the back of the chair, it was the responsibility of the actor to talk to the audience—a five-minute soliloquy with a spotlight directed on him—about why he committed the dastardly act that was the plot of the play. My drama coach told me that I could have that part if I promised *not* to stutter—at all (one of the worst things you can tell a stutterer)!

I told her with confidence that I could. However, I had no idea that I actually could because I was still a stutterer. But I stood by my promise and said my lines with such force that it masked my stuttering. Thankfully, the one-act play was held on only one night because I question whether I could have done it well twice! Well—I did it, and received applause at the conclusion of my soliloquy. It was a great night for a stutterer, giving me confidence to continue on my way to greater fluency!

We Must Prepare Ourselves

We have to *prepare* ourselves to feel comfortable in front of an audience. That means sometimes placing ourselves in uncomfortable situations in front of the public whether it be singing, acting, dancing, or engaging in disk jockey "patter" between songs on the radio. But many people are not singers, dancers, have the opportunity to act on stage, or be a radio announcer. So we look for other ways to practice our stage presence and speaking ability.

There are always other ways—other outlets. That means finding avenues for public speaking or at least exposure to the public. They can include:

1. Reading scripture for church services

2. Making announcements at meetings

3. Giving the treasurer's report for the organization to which you belong

4. Giving the announcements for the next week's activities

5. Volunteering to introduce the guest speaker at your organization's monthly meetings

6. Moving up the presentation ladder by giving a brief presentation at your next state conference or convention.

There are many ways through which we can give ourselves confidence in the arena of public speaking. Toastmasters clubs are a wonderful way to engage in public speaking in a relatively non-threatening environment.

Applause

Let's talk about organizing your presentation so that the audience will applaud when you conclude your remarks—not applauding because you are finally finished, but rather that you did a great job and inspired them! Toogood[1] presents some excellent suggestions. They are:

1. Begin with the Ending

Instead of beginning with, "Today I would like to speak about..." give the audience the premise of your presentation. For example:

> As I was walking from my car to this auditorium this afternoon, I noticed a young man sitting on the sidewalk next to this very building. He was holding a Styrofoam cup in his hand, asking for money to buy food. He was a nice looking young man, and certainly seemed to have the potential to be doing something more than begging for money. Reluctantly, I did place $2.00 in his cup

(smile somewhat sheepishly). But his situation was a perfect example of what I came to talk with you about today—rebuilding the industrial infrastructure of our city that will increase the opportunity for jobs for those in our community who have the ability to work! That young man obviously seemed able to work. I asked him if he had a job. His only response was that he could not find work. He had looked, but now it had come down to begging for money for the purpose of buying food!

That beginning had a much greater impact than "I have come to you today to discuss the industrial infrastructure of our city." With that introduction, audible snoring will probably be heard within the first 15 minutes of your presentation!

Of course, you are not always going to find the perfect example waiting for you outside of the building where you will be speaking. But what I am saying here is that an example used for the purpose of beginning your presentation or a story to exemplify in a more dramatic way what you came to say is a perfect way to begin your presentation. You are sounding a wakeup call to your audience, grabbing their attention so that they will continue listening to you!

Another example comes from a class that was entitled, "The New Testament—History and Social Climate" that I took while I was an undergraduate in college. The professor walked into our class on the first day and without pausing began by saying in all seriousness:

The course for which you have enrolled is about a girl, only about 13 years of age, who, in about the year One B.C., got herself pregnant and made up a spectacular story about being visited by an angel whose name was Gabriel who said that she would become pregnant without actually having sex! She called it an "immaculate conception." And people believed her! After giving birth to a baby boy, her story has remained to this day, and as a result many books have even been written about it including half of the Bible! And the birth even eventually developed a new religion called Christianity, all from that story she created in order to keep from getting herself in trouble or, in that era, put to death!

The class was taught at a conservative church-supported college. The course was taught primarily for those who were pre-ministerial students. When the professor finished that introduction, most of the students in the classroom had eyes about the size of half-dollars, mouths open, wondering what had prompted a professor who was a scholar of religious history to tell such a preposterous story!

The professor finally admitted that he was just kidding, of course, but it certainly grabbed everyone's attention! From that point on, the course centered on debunking his initial theory of the nativity that he had simply told in jest. And it worked!

In other words, the best way to grab your audience is to give them a wakeup call—something that is going to grab their attention and hold it while you build into your presentation. It works! And you will be considered a better public presenter than you thought you were!

2. *Use a Quotation to Begin Your Presentation*

The following is an example that is worth sharing here. That is, in the right setting a good quote that actually helps make your point can be what your presentation needs. Here is the example:

> *Thomas Jefferson once said that the great joy of being an American is simply having freedom of choice.... Well, I am sure that if Jefferson were alive today, he would certainly agree that at no time in our history have we had more chance to choose our future opportunities. I am talking about the abundance of opportunities that await us.*[2]

Such a quote will not only alert the audience to the topic of your presentation, but will also give it life. You have used a quote that is not only trustworthy, because it comes from Thomas Jefferson, but one that leads to the topic of your presentation.

3. Use a Rhetorical Question

This seems to not only bring an audience to attention, perhaps another wakeup call, but also can lead nicely into your presentation. Something like:

> *Why aren't we as a society accepting the fact that we live in a world in which Caucasians are becoming the racial minority? As we develop our businesses or develop new industry, are we keeping this fact at the forefront of our thinking?*
>
> *Why should we? The answer is this....*

A good rhetorical question will not only alert the audience to what you will be talking about, but will start them thinking about "Why?" and they will be listening to you to find the answer.

4. Project into the Future

Steve Jobs said it wonderfully when he declared, *"The ones who are crazy enough to think that they can change the world are the ones who do."* He did, indeed, change the world into what we know today. He was a "seer," one who looked into the future and saw possibilities that others did not see.

Toogood gives a good example of how to look into the future and grab your audience: *"Thirty years from now, the company you work for probably will not exist!"*[3] Now, that would be a great wakeup call to an audience of businesspeople!

5. *Look into the Past*

Use an example of what existed in the past and how that will in all probability impact on our future. There are similarities and differences in our history that can impact on us in the future. Take, for example, global warming. Fifty years ago, there was no mention of melting glaciers and rising oceans and the impact it could have on states such as Florida and California. If a speaker who is addressing a conference on the business climate in Miami, Florida began his speech by saying, *"If nothing is done to combat global warming, Miami, Florida will probably be under water by the year 2025. What will that do to the business climate in Miami? Businesses won't exist!"* that would certainly get the attention of those in attendance at that conference! It may have been a more dramatic first statement than one wants to hear. However, if that possibility did exist, it would make a great impact on the audience!

6. *Humor*

Some of the poorest beginnings to a speech involve humor. If you are not Bob Hope or Jerry Seinfeld, then don't risk it! A bad joke is not an ice breaker. But it can certainly "break up" an otherwise potentially impressive presentation (no pun intended). If you are going to use a humorous story to begin a speech, tell it as though it is true. Don't tell it as a joke. It can reduce the effectiveness of your presentation more than almost any other thing you can do.

Remember, the beginning of your speech is an extremely important component of your presentation.

Make it a *powerful* introduction, one that the audience will remember even if they don't remember anything else you say.

7. *Never Begin with an Apology!*

Never begin with an apology, such as, "I've never been much of a public speaker, but…" or "As I was driving over here today, I was trying to decide what I am going to say and wasn't able to come up with anything strikingly brilliant. Well…but I'll give it a try anyway."

I think I would consider leaving the auditorium at that point, wouldn't you?

Presenting Your Speech

In Chapter One of this book, I spoke to the topic of fear as it pertains to making public presentations. I'm not going reiterate that topic, but a statement by Steve Brown is pertinent here. He paraphrases an old saying, *"Cowards die a thousand deaths because they are constantly visualizing their dying."* He continues by saying, *"It is the same way with speeches. If you persist in visualizing your speech bombing, even if it doesn't you will have at least gone through the experience! Instead, visualize your speech being a tremendous success, and it very well may be one!"*[4]

Remember, success does breed success! The more you experience success in the process of speech making, and if you take it seriously, the better you will become.

An Exceptional Presenter

What does it take to be an exceptional presenter? That sounds like a very tough task. But if we want to be one, we need to know what is involved. So, what is an exceptional presenter? According to Koegel,[5] an exceptional presenter is:

1. *Organized*

Exceptional presenters take charge! They look poised and polished. They sound prepared. They are not there to waste time. Their goal is not to overwhelm but to inform, persuade, influence, entertain, or enlighten. Their message is well structured, well organized, and clearly defined.

2. *Passionate*

Exceptional presenters exude enthusiasm and conviction. It the presenter doesn't look and sound passionate about her or his topic, why should anyone else be passionate about it? Exceptional presenters speak from the heart and leave no doubt as to where they stand. Their energy is persuasive and contagious.

3. *Engaging*

Exceptional presenters do everything in their power to engage each member of the audience. They build rapport quickly and involve the audience early and often. If you want respect, you must first connect.

4. *Natural*

An exceptional presenter's style is *natural.* Their delivery has a conversational feel. Natural presenters make it look easy. They appear comfortable with the audience. A presenter who appears natural appears confident.

5. *Understand Your Audience*

Koegel stresses, as I stated earlier, that as an exceptional presenter you must understand your audience. He states that exceptional presenters learn as much as they can about their audience before presenting to them. The more you know about your audience, the easier it will be to connect and engage.

6. *Owning the Room*

He continues by talking about "owning the room." *Owning the room*, a phrase that I have used previously, is a term that describes stage actors and comedians, for example, who can "work" the stage with absolute confidence. She owns the room! Owning the room is what will happen for you once you have developed an open communication style. You will present with confidence and maintain the highest level of professionalism even in the most challenging circumstances.

I referred to Bill Clinton earlier in this book. He is an example of where good presentation skills can take you. In both his 1992 and 1996 presidential campaigns, he truly outscored both George H. Bush and Bob Dole. According to Koegel, from the first question of his first presidential debate, Bill Clinton owned the room. When the first question was directed to him, he looked the woman who asked it straight in the eye and asked her to tell him her name. Somewhat surprised, she told him. Then he answered her question. He was confident, and he was *connecting* with them. And those who were asking the questions knew it!

The Poorest Public Speakers

It is interesting to me that among the poorest public speakers seem to be those who are professionals presenting on stage at conferences and conventions. They typically appear to exhibit the poorest posture, the poorest stage presence, the poorest use of the microphone, and the poorest use of voice and speech patterns. They are difficult to understand, they speak so rapidly that a typical central nervous system cannot keep up with their sentence utterances, and they speak as though they are afraid to use the microphone properly or were never taught how to use it. They are the ones who know most about what they are presenting. They know the subject matter, and one would think that they would present in such a way that those in the audience would not have to struggle to hear and understand what they are saying! Or, as I said earlier, not have to struggle to stay awake!

The Problem Is...

The problem is that the majority of professionals in many fields have never been taught how to present information to an audience. The ability to be a polished public speaker might seem to them as something that comes naturally, without practice or rehearsal, or worst of all as something that doesn't require instruction on the fine points of presenting in public!

The remaining chapters of this book will present important information on topics that are critical to your effectiveness as a public speaker, including:

1. The art of using a microphone

2. The art of stage presence and manner of presentation

3. The art of concluding your presentation—making an impact!

These are all critical elements that will give you the skills to become a polished public speaker. Again, presenting in public is a performing art. As I, in so many words, said earlier in this chapter, you are the artist and the stage is your canvas. You are the one who can create a masterpiece! I know you can do it!

Notes

1. Toogood, *The Articulate Executive*.

2. Ibid., 38.

3. Ibid.

4. Brown, *How To Talk So People Will Listen.*

5. Timothy J. Koegel, *The Exceptional Presenter* (Austin, TX: Greenleaf Book Group Press, 2007).

CHAPTER SIX

THE PRIORITY OF PRESENTATION

By Jim Stovall

The most important part of any presentation is the message. All that any presenter can hope for is to accurately deliver the message to the audience. A message must be concise, clear, and specific. Being motivating, inspiring, or entertaining is not a message.

A great platform speaker once told me that "If you do a great job onstage, you will be lucky if your audience retains three ideas when they get out to the parking lot." I have found this to be true over the last several decades.

Most presenters try to deliver far too many aspects or points of their message. I find it helpful to simply tell my audience what it is that I want them to take away from our time together. I tell those who I present to specifically, "There are two things that you may or may not have known when you came into this auditorium today that I want to make sure you know when you leave." If there is a specific takeaway to your presentation, don't be afraid to label it as such.

There are two basic types of presenters. There are professional presenters who can speak to virtually any topic given a chance to do some research; and then there are passion presenters who would never stand up in front of an audience for any reason except for the single cause or message that they are totally committed to. Great presenters, actors, or platform speakers can technically fill any role.

My company, the Narrative Television Network, makes movies and television accessible for 13 million blind and visually-impaired Americans and millions more around the world. When we first launched the network in the early 1990s, to create programming and fill airtime I hosted a talk show and interviewed many of the classic film stars who were in the movies we narrated for our special audience. I remember the day I got to interview the great film star Jack Lemmon. Mr. Lemmon was known for many great roles including working with his lifelong friend and colleague Walter Matthau on the Broadway stage and movie version of Neil Simon's story *The Odd Couple.*

One of the most fascinating things I learned from my time talking with Mr. Lemmon was the fact that when he and Walter Matthau were doing eight shows a week on the Broadway stage for many consecutive months, they would often break up the monotony by taking the Sunday night performance and switching roles. If you ever saw the two of them embody their parts in *The Odd Couple*—either onstage or onscreen—you would have to agree that Lemmon and Matthau were perfectly casted actors for their individual parts. It is a tribute to their skills as actors and presenters that they could literally switch parts once a week and still make the play work.

Great courtroom attorneys often practice their presentation by arguing their own side of the case. Then they will switch and practice arguing their opponent's side of the same case.

A good presenter, given facts and details, can discuss the mating ritual of snow geese, explore the erosion rate around the Great Pyramids, or argue the benefits and drawbacks of the Industrial Revolution. Presenting is like acting. It is a skill that can be learned and developed.

I have had seven of my books turned into movies. I have had the privilege of having characters I have created embodied by legendary actors such as James Garner, Peter

Fonda, Raquel Welch, Academy Award winner Louis Gossett Jr., and many others.

I remember working on casting for the movie version of my novel entitled *The Lamp*. *The Lamp* story features a mysterious character somewhat like a magic genie who emerges from an ugly garage-sale lamp. My first thought was to have Barbara Eden play the part. Many fans of classic TV will remember Barbara Eden starring in *I Dream of Jeannie*. I thought it would be a fun parody to have her playing a genie-like character again almost a half century after she was introduced as a genie in her original role.

Fortunately, or unfortunately, when I met Barbara Eden it was immediately apparent that the parody would not work because she is still a classically beautiful woman, and the parody would have been lost on our movie audience.

Next, I thought we could make it a comical character, and I thought of the zany antics of Tim Conway. Anyone who saw Mr. Conway's comic sketches on *The Carol Burnett Show* will never forget his performances. I talked with Mr. Conway, and while I was confident in his skill and professionalism, I feared that his comedic presence could take away from the gravity of the character.

Finally, I thought of the legendary Academy Award-winning performer Louis Gossett Jr. of *An Officer and a Gentleman* fame. For over 50 years, Mr. Gossett has been a commanding presence on the stage as well as the screen. I remain very pleased and grateful that we chose Louis Gossett Jr. and that he was willing to bring his immense talent to *The Lamp* movie. As great as Mr. Gossett was in that role, I believe Barbara Eden or Tim Conway could have done an equally great job. It just would have been very different.

Great actors, performers, or presenters are skilled at delivering messages to audiences; however, the best among them will tell you they always prefer to deliver a message that matters to them personally. If you want to make a great presentation, begin with a message that matters deeply to you.

I recently saw a mother whose child had been killed by a drunk driver. She was making a presentation for the wonderful organization *Mothers Against Drunk Drivers*. No one would consider this particular mother as a great traditional presenter simply by considering her stage presence or presenting skills; however, her undying commitment to the cause about which she was presenting made all the difference.

As a professional speaker, broadcaster, columnist, movie producer, and author, I am fortunate that some past success has given me the freedom to create and deliver messages that matter to me personally. I could write a book or make a speech on almost any topic, but my presentation would lose some of the passion that comes with delivering a message that matters to me.

In the 1990s, a trend emerged in corporate America involving every organization developing a mission statement. While I believe a quality mission statement can be a rallying point for any organization, I fear that far too many corporations wasted time and money developing their mission statement and then simply posted the statement on the wall and forgot about it.

Being a great presenter involves a message that is tied to one's own life mission. It doesn't really matter if your mission is personal or professional, because if the passion is high enough the two have a tendency to merge together.

I think it is critical for every highly-evolved, passionate person to have their own individual mission statement. Mine was ironically developed for me by my grandmother. While she had never been involved with any formal business enterprise or area of presenting, she was able to pinpoint and articulate my passion.

Late in my grandmother's life, she had medical care provided for her in her home. Our family knew that her time was short, so we all took every opportunity to visit her. I remember stopping by her home—several hundred miles from where I live—during a trip between two speaking engagements. I arrived late one night and was disappointed to learn from her nurse that my grandmother had already fallen asleep.

The nurse was very kind to me and said, "Your grandmother is very proud of you and all that you do." I told her that I wasn't even sure if my grandmother knew what I did. The nurse replied, "There's a framed picture of you holding your Emmy Award sitting on the night stand next to her bed. She tells everyone who comes to see her about her grandson who does two things. He helps blind people see television, and he tells people around the world that they can have good things in their lives."

The minute those words—relayed from my grandmother through her nurse—registered in my brain, I knew that I had my mission statement and my message.

I am often called on by corporations for whom I am speaking to customize my presentation to deal with a specific aspect of their business. I gladly do this, but those customized points are always clearly wrapped in my passion involving the message I feel responsible for delivering.

I believe we are all put here on earth to find our individual gifts, and our purpose in life involves giving our gifts to others.

If you are going to make presentations that matter to you both now and in the future, they have to involve your passion. My passion for the Narrative Television Network and accessible programming came out of my own need and disability. One of the most unique forms of presenting is to make someone else's presentation accessible to an audience who otherwise would not have been able to benefit from it or enjoy it.

Immediately after losing my sight and realizing that I would live the rest of my life as a blind person, I didn't write bestselling books, make movies, write newspaper columns, make speeches, or any of the other activities that occupy my time today. That morning I woke up and realized that I had lost the remainder of my sight, I moved into a little nine-by-twelve-foot room in the back of my house where I gathered my radio, my telephone, and my tape recorder. That little room became my whole world 25 years ago. The thought of traveling millions of miles and presenting to millions of people via the outlets I utilize today would have seemed as foreign to me then as going to the moon.

Fortunately as I look back on that time prior to losing my sight, that little room in the back of my house was our television room. That was where we enjoyed broadcast and cable TV as well as the numerous classic movies I kept there in my collection. I have always been a huge fan of classic movie stars, which has made the opportunity to have many of my novels turned into films very gratifying.

One day as a totally blind person sitting in my little room that I thought I would never leave again, I became bored and decided to play one of my classic movies. Even though I knew I couldn't see it any more, I thought I had watched that particular movie so many times I should be able to just listen to the sound track and follow along with the story. I had selected an old Humphrey Bogart movie entitled *The Big Sleep* that I had enjoyed countless times.

My idea of following along just by listening worked for a while, but then somebody shot someone, someone else screamed, and a car sped away as I totally forgot what happened next in the plot of the movie. I got really frustrated and said the magic words, "Somebody ought to do something about that."

The next time you get frustrated and hear yourself say, "Somebody ought to do something about that," you just had a great idea. The whole world is hoping and praying for a great idea, and they trip over one about three times each week.

The only thing you've got to do to have a great idea is to go through your daily routine, wait for something bad to happen, and ask yourself, "How could I have avoided that?" The answer to that question is a great idea.

To take it one step further, the only thing you have to do to have a great business opportunity is to ask yourself, "How can I help other people avoid that problem?" The answer to that question represents a great business opportunity.

Everyone wants to make money when the only people who make money work at the U.S. Mint printing dollar bills. The rest of us have to earn money, and we must remember that money is only earned by creating value in the lives of other people. If you're going to pursue a passion and deliver presentations that are significant and fulfilling, you need to make sure you are meeting the needs of other people.

Out of my frustration with the Humphrey Bogart movie, I—along with some very talented and dedicated colleagues—created a great business and an entire industry. We at the Narrative Television Network make movies and TV programs accessible to millions of blind and visually impaired people and their families by adding the voice of a narrator to the programming's soundtrack between the dialogue of the characters. This additional narration describes the actions, settings, and other visual elements of the program.

Beyond the work we do for network TV and movie programming, we find it extremely gratifying to be able to make hundreds of hours of educational programming accessible to blind and visually impaired students allowing them to learn and study alongside their sighted classmates.

Presentations can involve your own thoughts and ideas as well as the thoughts and ideas of others repackaged, reinterpreted, or made accessible. People who translate the work of others into various languages—along with presenters who make the complex principles of others' work understandable—all provide a valuable service and can create powerful presentations.

If you are going to make a presentation utilizing someone else's original work, thoughts, ideas, or experiences as the foundation of your message, you need to employ a technique I call *putting yourself in the picture*. Putting yourself in the picture involves creating a connection between the message and your presentation that involves you.

This is why I have played a cameo role in each of the movies based on my novels. If you have a chance to catch any of the films based on my books, and if you don't blink, you will catch a brief scene with a limousine driver, a bartender, or some other insignificant character in the story. That bartender, limo driver, or other insignificant character will look just like me. I am willing to play anything in the movies except a blind guy, which is why I started my cameo acting career as a limo driver.

The result of putting myself in the movies has been the benefit of putting myself and my audience in the picture when I write about or make presentations involving concepts or messages from my movies.

Recently, I heard an interview on the radio about the curator of a local art museum discovering a valuable painting that everyone in the art world had believed to be missing for over a century. I thought this discovery or re-discovery could make an interesting story, novel, movie, or the basis for a point I might want to make in a personal development book or speech.

Instead of presenting it to my audience as simply something I heard about, which anyone listening to the radio that day could have done, I called the museum, interviewed the curator, and made arrangements to tour the museum's vault and actually touch the painting that had been lost for over a century. Now I can present to my audience something that has happened to me and not just something I heard about.

One of my favorite American authors, Louis L'Amour, wrote over 100 novels involving the American West. He was fond of saying, "If I write about a mountain, I've climbed it; if I describe a trail, I've walked on it; and if my characters cross a stream, I have waded through it myself."

I believe putting himself in the picture made Mr. L'Amour's writing more personal and vivid to his readers and may well be one of the reasons he is among the best-selling authors of the twentieth century.

You've probably heard about the parlor game *The Six Degrees of Kevin Bacon,* which involves connecting two actors who have never worked together via colleagues they have each worked with in separate films. We live in a connected world, and given the current advantages of social media there's no person, place, or thing you can't connect to, allowing you to put yourself and your audience in the picture when you're making your presentation.

If you're driving down the street and you see a Little League baseball game in progress, you might glance that direction for a few moments; but if the game includes your child or grandchild, it's a whole other matter. Owning your message and creating passion for your audience is the key to creating transformational presentations.

CHAPTER SEVEN

THE ART OF USING
A MICROPHONE

By Ray Hull, PhD

The proper use of a microphone is critical when making
a public presentation. A good microphone and PA system
used correctly can improve an otherwise poorly designed
auditorium, meeting room, or church sanctuary into one
that will enhance an audience's ability to hear you well. In
fact, the proper use of a well-designed PA system is critical

to being heard! Why else are you there in the first place? You want to be heard! But we also have to understand that a well-used microphone and PA system will never improve a speaker who does not speak well! On the other hand, a speaker who speaks well, says something worth hearing, and knows how to use a microphone and PA system will definitely be appreciated by their audience.

Microphones Don't Bite!

As I stated in the book entitled *The Art of Communication* authored by Jim Stovall and myself, I find it amusing when I observe a speaker who is handed a microphone so that she or he can be heard by the audience, but the hand that was given the microphone is suddenly dropped to the waist or held at arm's length in front of the chest. The speaker seems to be attempting to keep the microphone as far away as possible from her or his mouth. When asked to hold the microphone closer to the mouth so that the speaker can be heard, the speaker may be seen to gingerly bring it closer, as though the microphone may bite if it comes too close!

Another microphone problem occurs when a lapel microphone is pinned to a speaker's shirt, tie, or blouse. It seems all too frequently to be placed at or around the area of the speaker's belt or near the bottom of the necktie, not realizing that at that distance from the speaker's mouth it will not respond to their voice. Or, when a speaker is asked to speak from a podium on which a flexible "goose-neck" is attached that holds a well-designed microphone, speakers seem all too frequently to move as far away as possible and then are not heard by the audience! At any distance beyond around five inches, a typical stage microphone will not respond to the speaker's voice, and therefore the speaker will probably not be heard. How sad it is that a speaker who came to present an important message appears to either not want to be heard or simply does not know how to use a microphone properly!

Why Don't Speakers Want to Use a Microphone?

It is interesting, but rather sad, to observe speakers who walk to the podium and say directly into the microphone that they are happy to be there, and then promptly walk away from the podium and the microphone as though they do not realize that the microphone was placed there so that the audience can hear what they have to say. It is further disturbing to hear them say directly into the microphone, "I won't need to use the microphone because people can always hear what I am saying without one." I tell my audiences to raise their hand and say loudly, "*Please* use the microphone so we can hear you!"

One of my patients confessed to me that she had gone to a meeting of her local Audubon Society one evening. She had looked forward to attending, but arrived a little later than she had intended. So she took the only seat that was available, about ten rows back from the front, on the isle. When the speaker was introduced, the speaker walked to the podium and said clearly into the microphone that she was pleased to be there, and then promptly walked around in front of the podium while saying, "I am sure that I won't need to use the microphone because my voice is easily heard without one." My patient said that there were over 100 people in the audience, and hardly any of them could hear a word she said for the next hour! I asked her, "Did anyone say something to her—to please use the microphone?"

She said "No."

I then asked her, "Why didn't you ask her to use the microphone?"

She quietly responded, "I didn't want to be a bother. After all, I'm just an old lady who doesn't hear as well as I used to."

It is sad and sometimes disturbing to me when a speaker such as the one described above apparently either does not know or does not care that the audience will in all probability not hear what she is saying. It is equally sad that those in the audience, in this instance, did not have the courage to say, "Please use the microphone so we can hear you!"

Don't we want to be heard?

To me, it is difficult to comprehend why, if we are speaking in front of an audience, we would not want our audience to hear what we are saying! We should *want* to be heard! Why else are we there? It is frustrating when I observe a speaker who is in front of an audience that is obviously there for the purpose of hearing what the speaker has to say, but the speaker is apparently attempting to "hide" from the audience because they seem to be afraid to use a microphone! It doesn't matter if we are speaking before an audience of 500 or simply reading the minutes of the previous meeting or the financial report at a gathering of a local civic organization. The proper use of a microphone is essential for effective public speaking! But perhaps the speaker doesn't know how to use it properly.

How Does a Microphone Work?

There is nothing magical about microphones. They are simply a mechanical/electroacoustic device that responds to sound pressure—our voice. They respond to sound by giving it a little boost and then sending the voice signal on to an amplifier of a PA system that the microphone is attached to in order to boost one's voice further. It is as simple (and complicated) as that!

Are There Different Types of Microphones?

Types of microphones are many. They include *dynamic microphones*; *condenser microphones*; *high impedance microphones*; *low impedance microphones*; *wireless microphones* that transmit sound by way of an FM (frequency modulation) signal to an FM receiver within the amplifier; *hard-wire microphones* that are hard-wired directly to the amplifier; *lapel microphones* that are pinned to the speaker's shirt, blouse, or necktie; and *microphones that are affixed to a podium* by way of a holder that is screwed permanently onto the podium, usually called a "gooseneck" because it is rather long and flexible. If the speaker desires to use notes or desires the security of standing behind the podium, then this type can be useful.

What Does the Microphone Do?

Microphones, if used properly, do their job of transmitting one's voice to the auditorium's amplifier and public address system so that the audience can hear the speaker's voice comfortably.

The majority of microphones found in auditoriums, meeting rooms, churches, and other environments where people gather are *high impedance microphones.*

What is a high impedance microphone? If you know what the term "to impede" means, then you have an idea of what the microphone does. They are specifically designed to impede, or restrict, the speaker's or singer's voice so that other sounds or other pieces of amplifying equipment in the vicinity of the stage do not interfere with the speaker or singer's voice. For example, the irritating squeal that can be heard through a PA system when there are other amplifiers on the stage behind the speaker or singer will be reduced or eliminated. That is one of the specific reasons that auditoriums, church sanctuaries, and other meeting rooms use high impedance microphones. The microphones serve a dual purpose in order to accommodate speakers, singers, and other musicians.

The primary reason for the design that impedes the speech or music signal is simple functionality. Sound engineers have designed high impedance microphones to restrict stray electrical and acoustic signals from being picked up by the microphone, causing that irritating squeal referred to above.

How Should I Use a Microphone?

Remember, microphones are there to help, not to hinder! And they do not bite!

As I said earlier, most churches, auditoriums, and meeting rooms are equipped with high impedance microphones, so it is imperative that speakers be knowledgeable regarding their use. Those microphones restrict or impede the sounds of speech or the voice of a singer, so the speaker's mouth must not be more than four to five inches from the microphone. That is critical if the speaker is going to use the microphone as it was intended to be used. Otherwise, the microphone will not do what it is designed to do. That is, give the speaker or singer's voice the intensity and clarity that it deserves!

As I said in the book *The Art of Communication* by Jim Stovall and myself, "That is where the fear factor comes into play. Don't be afraid! The microphone is guaranteed *not* to bite!"

Lapel Microphones

If a lapel microphone is given to you or someone is in charge of pinning it on to your necktie, shirt, or blouse, it is frequently up to you to make sure that it is pinned in the correct location. Make sure that for men it is pinned to your collar or the top of the necktie and *not* the bottom of your shirt or necktie. If you are a woman and you happen to have worn your new rather low-neck dress, ask for a scarf of some type and have the person in charge pin the microphone up near your chin. Or, better yet, ask ahead of time about the type of microphone you will be using. You might avoid being embarrassed.

Podium Microphones

If a microphone is attached to a podium by way of what is called a "gooseneck" holder, you usually have a choice. If it is designed properly, you can remove the microphone from the holder and use it as a hand-held microphone. That is what I prefer because I do not like to be confined to a podium. I want to stand away from the podium so that the audience can see me. If the microphone is permanently attached to the microphone holder, then you can stand so that the microphone is no further than four to five inches from your mouth, which may require that you lean forward just a little.

Hand-Held Microphones

I prefer a hand-held microphone so that I can control its distance and position. Best of all is an FM hand-held microphone. They generally have better quality and are very mobile. On the other hand, if the location where you are speaking does not possess an FM system, then a hard-wire system is just fine. Just make sure that the wire that attaches the microphone to the amplifier and speaker system does not become tangled around your feet. That can become rather embarrassing while the audience watches you try to untangle the wire from your feet! So keep the microphone in one hand, hold the wire in the other, and keep it away from your feet.

Experiment Beforehand

I mentioned earlier that the microphone should be no further than four to five inches from the speaker's mouth. But it is best to experiment before you begin your presentation, and if possible do that before the audience arrives. If part of the audience is already sitting in the meeting room or auditorium, use them as your rehearsal audience before you begin. Experiment with the positioning of the microphone and ask them if they can hear you clearly. If not, then move a little closer to the microphone, or move the microphone closer to you, and ask again. If they say that you are too loud, then move the microphone away an inch or two. Adjust until the sound of your voice is perfect, and remember the distance that was best. Use those who arrived early as your "sound checkers" as you are adjusting the position of the microphone in relation to you and your mouth. It generally works wonderfully.

A Final Word on Microphone Use

As I said earlier, the proper use of the microphone is *critical* to effective public speaking. You can have the most powerful speech ever presented, and you may be an excellent speaker. But if the audience cannot hear you, your message will be lost. If your voice is over-amplified and the intensity of your voice is so loud that it is uncomfortable, the audience will not be listening to you because they will spend the time of your presentation wondering "Why doesn't someone turn that #$%& PA system down!"

On the other hand, you may have developed a wonderful speech, but if you are standing 18 inches from the podium microphone and the microphone cannot pick up your voice, again the message will likewise be lost somewhere within the 18-inch void between your mouth and the microphone, floating around that small space and unheard by the audience.

The microphone is there to promote you and what *you* have to say! It is there to respond to the sound of your voice—your words. To allow the PA system to do its job and let the audience hear *you,* learn to use it correctly! It is a wonderful device that is there to be used correctly by those who want to be heard!

CHAPTER EIGHT

PARTS OF THE PRESENTATION

By Jim Stovall

If you surveyed any cross section of people in the world and asked them the most fearful environment or situation they can imagine, a high percentage of people would respond with an answer involving standing onstage to give a speech or make a presentation. While as a professional speaker myself I would have to acknowledge this fear, it's important to realize we can minimize the discomfort and intimidation if we will simply address every part of the presentation and create our own home court advantage. A home court advantage in sports or in the world of presenting involves making the unknown, frightening situation as familiar and comfortable as possible.

I have been an entrepreneur for over 25 years, involved in running a number of ventures and business operations. In our litigious business environment here in the twenty-first century, I am pleased to be able to say I have never sued anyone or been sued by anyone; however, I have had to testify as an expert witness in several trials.

Before I went to testify in federal court for the first time I was talking with my own corporate attorney, and I shared with him that I was a bit nervous about having to appear in court as an expert witness. As he is now an octogenarian having practiced law for over half a century, he is generally full of advice regarding everything in and around the courtroom.

He suggested that I go to the courtroom where I would be testifying to experience the atmosphere while another trial was going on. Then he also recommended that I arrive in court early the day of my testimony in order to walk around the courtroom and sit in the witness box before anyone else arrived. I heeded my lawyer's advice and had a much more relaxed and comfortable experience testifying than I otherwise would have had. I recommend that all speakers and presenters do their own prep work and walkthrough before the presentation.

As a blind person myself, I always travel to the venue for my speeches with one of my assistants. For each arena event or corporate speech, we make arrangements to arrive at a time when we can do a walkthrough onstage before the scheduled time for my speech. This gives me the chance to count my steps, visualize any barriers or obstacles, and generally get the feeling of the site before my audience arrives. Although this is a necessity for me as a blind person, it can become a valuable asset for any presenter.

It is a valuable exercise to not only familiarize yourself with the venue from the stage or podium perspective but to also get the feeling of the venue from the perspective of several points in the audience. All arenas, convention centers, and outdoor venues are different. They each have their own feel, sound, and atmosphere. Never take any of it for granted.

Also familiarize yourself with backstage accommodations and take the opportunity to meet as many of the event staff and crew as possible. Always check and double check the microphone. Find out if they have a backup and how you would make the switch in the event of a microphone failure. Determine whether you prefer a podium microphone, a lavalier mic, or a handheld.

There are advantages and disadvantages to each. Podium microphones are fixed in one spot and are generally the most stable and reliable. Lavalier mics that attach to your clothing or are worn over your ear with an unobtrusive extension near your mouth offer great freedom and flexibility but can develop static or interference as they utilize wireless technology.

I prefer a handheld microphone as a general rule whether it has a cord or is cordless. A handheld mic offers most of the stability and reliability of a podium mic but a lot of the freedom of a lavalier setup. If you are prone to allergies or are suffering from a cold or sore throat, a handheld mic also gives you the ability to move the mic away from you if you cough or sneeze. This can be a challenge if you're wearing a lavalier microphone.

During your walkthrough, verify how the microphone sounds throughout the venue and determine the best distance to have between you and the microphone. Always check where the mic will be when you walk onstage, and confirm that it will be turned on before you are introduced or as you are walking to the podium.

Determine whether your presentation is going to be video or audio recorded and what the parameters are for the use of that recording. Check whether the house mic will be the audio for the recording or whether there will be an auxiliary microphone. Check with the crew on the lighting that will be used during your presentation, and be sure to stay in the lighted area as you can disappear from view very quickly if you veer out of the lit portion of the platform. If you are being video recorded or projected via IMAG equipment, be sure to know how far from center stage you can move without adversely impacting the video.

If you are using a podium, determine whether the sound will resonate in the microphone if you touch or bump the podium. Many podiums have wheels or castors that make it easy to move them on and off the stage. Be sure the wheels or castors are locked down before your presentation or you may find yourself chasing after your podium.

If your presentation calls for slides or video images, double and triple check all equipment well in advance of your presentation. Spare slides, cords, and lightbulbs are all recommended. It may be next week, next month, or next year, but sooner or later, you will be very thankful for the backup equipment.

If you are able to control the temperature of the room where you are presenting, always make it slightly cooler than you would otherwise have it before your audience arrives. If it's too warm before your crowd enters the room, they will collectively warm it up far beyond where most venues have the ability to cool it off during the time of your presentation.

Try to know what other competing events or distracting activities may be going on at the site of your presentation. You will want to try to control interruptions or distractions as much as possible; however, life dictates that we can't control everything.

My late, great friend and mentor Coach John Wooden often said, "Things turn out best for those who make the best out of the way things turn out." I have had every imaginable distraction and interruption during my many years onstage. I remember speaking to an investment banking convention at an amphitheater in Memphis when right in the middle of my speech the lights went out. You may ask how I, as a blind person, even knew the lights went out. It's because as I was standing on the stage, I heard one of the backstage crew members say into his walkie-talkie, "We just lost all the lights in the house." My first goal was to avoid panic and potential injuries among the thousands of people in my audience. My second goal was to save my presentation and keep my message on track.

Humor is always your friend in these situations. It is impossible for an audience to panic while they are laughing. Standing on the stage in a darkened amphitheater filled with investment bankers, I paused for a couple of seconds and then calmly said, "Welcome to my world. Your meeting planner and corporate team thought of every possible detail and wanted you to experience this meeting from my perspective for a little while." The audience laughed, and I continued as if nothing had happened.

It was only a few minutes—even though it seemed like hours—before the lights came back on, and I finished the presentation without a hitch. It's not a matter of *if* something will go wrong. It's a matter of *when* something will go wrong, and you've got to make it work. The message and the mission are too important to allow your presentation to be ruined by a technical challenge.

People often ask me what meeting planners, event promoters, and speakers bureaus are looking for when they hire a high-priced professional speaker. It would surprise most people to learn that one of the most critical things they are looking for is someone who can finish right on time. It's important to be flexible with respect to how long your presentation will run.

When I'm asked to speak, they will invariably tell my staff how long they want me to talk, but I always disregard whatever they say and ask them what time they would like me to finish. If there has ever been a meeting, convention, or arena event that ran on time, it certainly wasn't one that I attended. I am invariably getting onstage either a little before or considerably after the schedule called for me to make my presentation. A presenter becomes very valuable if they can instantly adjust their material to get the whole event back on schedule.

Over the years, I have developed approximately three hours of material that I can use in a speech. I visualize my material in my mind like a train. I can add or subtract railroad cars from my train before my speech or even when I am presenting in order to fit whatever time parameters are required. If you want to get the reputation of a topflight professional speaker or presenter, learn how to always conclude your presentation at the right time.

Nothing will get your presentation off to a good start more than a great introduction, and nothing will have you struggling to dig yourself out of a difficult presentation hole more than a bad introduction. I take no chances on the content or quality of my introduction when I go to make a speech. My team and I have crafted what we feel is the optimal introduction for me through trial and error over the years. This is the actual introduction that we currently send to meeting planners, promoters, and masters of ceremonies before I speak.

Jim Stovall Introduction

In spite of blindness, Jim Stovall has been a National Olympic weightlifting champion, a successful investment broker, the President of the Emmy Award-winning Narrative Television Network, and a highly sought-after author and platform speaker. He is the author of 30 books, including the bestseller, The Ultimate Gift, which is now a major motion picture from 20th Century Fox starring James Garner and Abigail Breslin. Three of his other novels have also been made into movies with two more in production.

Steve Forbes, president and CEO of Forbes magazine, says, "Jim Stovall is one of the most extraordinary men of our era."

For his work in making television accessible to our nation's 13 million blind and visually impaired people, The President's Committee on Equal Opportunity selected Jim Stovall as the Entrepreneur of the Year. Jim Stovall has been featured in The Wall Street Journal, Forbes magazine, USA Today, and has been seen on Good Morning America, CNN, and CBS Evening News. He was also chosen as the International Humanitarian of the Year, joining Jimmy Carter, Nancy Reagan, and Mother Teresa as recipients of this honor.

Prior to every presentation, always send your current introduction to everyone involved with an event. Don't take any chances. Carry several extra copies with you to the venue. Find out who will be introducing you, and be sure to offer them one of your extra copies of the introduction immediately before your presentation. Remember, event planners and masters of ceremonies have a million things on their minds, and your introduction sheet may not be at the top of their list. Whether your introduction is lost, stolen, misplaced, or eaten like nonexistent homework by the proverbial dog, have a copy of your introduction handy at the critical moment.

Strongly request or politely demand that whomever is introducing you read the entire prepared introduction before your presentation. If they have extra remarks or comments they want to make about you or your presentation, ask them to do it before they read the prepared sheet.

After you've done everything possible to get a great introduction, be prepared for it all to go wrong as you may be walking onto the stage cold. This has happened to me, and my contingency is to thank my audience then say, "Twenty-five years ago when I woke up and discovered I had lost the remainder of my sight, I began living my life as a blind person, which involved moving into a little nine-by-twelve-foot room in the back of my house. If you had told me then everything that would happen to me including...." I insert a version of my own introduction into my speech at this point.

The most important elements of a great presentation are:

1. Who said it?

2. How well did they say it?

3. What did they say?

In order to maximize our message, the only tool we have to tell our audience who we are is our introduction.

As stated in an earlier chapter, you should contrast and punctuate emotion with humor throughout your presentation. You want it to be emotional without totally draining your audience, and you want it to be humorous but not to the point of becoming trivial. You must know your audience.

Days or weeks before your presentation, a good meeting planner or event coordinator can give you a profile or overview of who will be in your audience. Find out what is going on at their event and throughout their organization.

Be sure to know who is on before you so you can calibrate your presentation.

I have followed Jay Leno onstage. It is a different atmosphere than following other presenters I have worked with such as Zig Ziglar, Tony Robbins, Christopher Reeve, Colin Powell, or Barbara Bush. Understand how long your audience has been seated during the session you are presenting. The mind can only absorb what the rear end can endure.

I recommend that you always keep your language, demeanor, and content G or PG rated. I have never heard a presenter criticized for not using profanity, vulgarity, or off-color stories.

As I have previously mentioned, I have approximately three hours of material that I can mix and match onstage to create my presentation, but the opening three minutes of my speeches are always 100 percent memorized, canned, and rehearsed. There's already enough anxiety when you start a presentation without having to struggle for your opening lines. If you will have the opening of your presentation set in concrete, it will give you a few moments to settle down, relax, and get ready to deliver an impactful presentation.

I believe the most important part of any presentation is the call to action near the end of your time with your audience. This is when you can deliver the transformational "so what?" message that gives them their marching orders. It's important for your audience to realize that knowing something without doing something creates no results.

I always tell my audiences, "You can change your life when you change your mind." My speech will change their minds, but they have to take action to change their lives.

I am unusual among speakers, authors, and presenters in that I offer my audience and my readers—including you as a result of reading this book—a way to stay in touch with me: Jim@JimStovall.com. I have 10 million books in print and have spoken to millions of people at live events, and I give everyone, including you, an ongoing connection to me. I am not only committed to making powerful presentations, but I am also committed to being a part of the change that my audience and my readers are seeking.

Knowing something must always be followed by doing something. This is why our presentations must be both informational and motivational. Many people have information without action. They don't fail because they don't know what to do. They fail because they don't do what they know.

Commit to being a person of change in your own life, and through your presentations commit to offering positive change to the world.

CHAPTER NINE

THE ART OF STAGE PRESENCE AND MANNER OF PRESENTATION

By Ray Hull, PhD

As I said earlier in this book, presenting in public truly is an art form, or rather, a performing art. And if we intend to engage in it, it is imperative that we prepare to perform. Of course there are times when we are not speaking on stage; rather, it may be at a meeting or a civic or church organization. Wherever we perform, however, it is important that we are prepared by being well aware of the elements that comprise an excellent presenter.

Actors attend classes on the art of stage acting. They observe skilled actors and actresses to gain knowledge regarding their techniques. They strive to learn the skills that make them great.

Likewise, we can observe excellent presenters either in person or via video or on YouTube. We can watch and listen to John F. Kennedy's speeches when he was running for the presidency or during his brief time in office. We can watch and listen to Martin Luther King, Jr. and his great speeches. And while watching and listening to those, we might say, "I could never do that! I could never speak well enough to move an audience to action!" And we may never become that good of a public speaker. But we can learn the techniques that they used and can become a little better than we might have otherwise been.

My first position at a university involved teaching a course entitled Speech 101. It was a public speaking course at that university that was taken by all students. Most of them were in their freshman or sophomore year of college. I asked each of them on the first day of class to stand before the rest of the class and tell everyone something interesting about themselves. I did that in order to begin to get them used to addressing an audience, in this instance their fellow classmates. And I felt that topic should have been an easy one for them to speak about. As I listened to them, it was nearly always evident that I had my work cut out for me if any were going to become a credible public speaker. Of course there always seemed to be one or two who were either more outgoing than the rest of the class or possessed the self-confidence or experience that revealed some potential. I was happy to see potential for excellence in those few. For the majority, however, I could only hope that by the conclusion of the semester they would develop the ability to speak in such a way that they could be understood by their audience. Inevitably, the majority of the class would reach the end of the semester either as good as the potential they showed on the first day of class or as poor as they had revealed on that first day. A grade of "C" seemed to be the norm as far as grades were concerned for about 80 percent of the class.

It seemed that no matter how I instructed the students about stage presence, at the conclusion of the semester the majority would still be engaged in poor public presentation habits. Those included squirming and twisting rather than standing still when speaking, not knowing what to do with their hands, speaking so rapidly that they were difficult to understand, appearing as though they were studying the floor, and looking at the ceiling or the walls of the room rather than at their audience. Even with what I felt to be good instruction on effective presentation skills, at the conclusion of the semester the majority would continue to squirm, giggle, look at the floor, and speak so rapidly that we would have a hard time understanding what they were saying. It was quite defeating to say the least. I continue to hope that something that I instructed them to do during Speech 101 has stayed with them to help them to be the best public speaker that they can be. However, I have to wonder.

Stage Presence

Have you ever carefully watched a professional singer during their a performance, particularly when they are standing on stage alone? Have you observed their posture, their hands, the positioning of their feet, the movements of their head, the expression on their face, and their eye contact? If you have, did you notice all of those elements of their performance? If you did, or if you will, you will also notice the perfect stage presence of an excellent public speaker.

Excellent presenters don't wave their arms, pace back and forth across the stage, or talk loudly and rapidly. If you will find a Facebook video of a speech by John F. Kennedy or a speech by Barak Obama, you will notice the mannerisms of an excellent public speaker. Those include:

Posture

When a professional speaker stands before an audience, she or he does not pace back and forth. They stand still and speak directly to the audience. Their back is straight, but not so straight as to look stilted. Perhaps they will lean forward just a little in order to engage the audience, so that the audience knows that the speaker is speaking directly to them.

Positioning of the Feet

When a professional singer or a professional speaker walks onto the stage, they, as is also said in the world of the theater, will generally "own the audience." They are (or act) confident as they walk with purpose directly to where they intend to stand (usually in the middle of the stage), and they begin to talk to the audience—with confidence!

Have you watched how they position their feet? When an accomplished speaker or singer stops at the location where they intend to remain for their performance or their presentation, their feet are generally about 20 inches apart. They aren't standing with their feet in a "fighting" stance, wide apart and ready for the first punch (unless you are doing an Elvis Presley imitation)! Nor are their feet so close together that they appear to be that of a ballet dancer, and we wonder if they are going to fall over at some time during their presentation! Their feet are positioned comfortably, and they keep them in that position during their speech or their musical performance. They may move occasionally, but those movements will be used for a purpose. They do not move randomly around the stage when they are before their audience.

Hands

A professional singer or speaker will keep their hands at their side—not wildly gesturing or in their pockets. They are standing comfortably, again feet about 20 inches apart, perhaps leaning slightly forward, and with hands comfortably at their side. A moderate gesture for emphasis on occasion is appropriate, but for the majority of the time their hands are kept loosely at their side. We usually don't notice this because there is nothing to bring it to our attention, nor are there any distracting movements. Those excellent speakers or singers use their eyes, their face, their head movements, and their body positioning to present themselves and the emotion that they wish to express.

Eye Contact

Our eyes will frequently say more than we intend. As I said in the book *The Art of Communication* by Jim Stovall and myself, our eye movements are dead giveaways to what is going on in our mind. For example, a lack of eye contact or frequent glances to one side or another indicates serious disagreement, disinterest, extreme nervousness, or a thought-provoking "Why am I here!"

Eye contact during a presentation is seriously important. I tell my audiences that the best area of the face to focus on when speaking to an individual or to an audience is their nose. When I am speaking to an audience, no matter how large or small, I make eye contact with as many in the audience as I can by concentrating on their nose, one person at a time. By concentrating on their nose, it appears that we are concentrating only on that individual and no one else. They feel as though we are speaking only to them. We aren't looking into the person's eyes. That is too intimate. We are concentrating on the person's face—actually their nose. It is a comfortable location for both you and your audience.

Rate of Speech

I am sure that you already know this, but the majority of people in the U.S. and many other countries talk too fast! I become fatigued when listening to some speakers, including listening to some of my professors when I was in college, many pastors who preach on Sunday mornings, most politicians, car salespeople, television news broadcasters, and public speakers whom I listen to from time to time. Many of them speak so rapidly that it becomes difficult to understand all of the words that they are saying. I actually despise listening to certain people who appear to take delight in speaking "trippingly on the tongue"!

Occasionally I am asked to work with news broadcasters and other public speakers about whom radio or television stations receive complaints from listeners or viewers because they are having difficulty understanding what they are saying. When I work with them, one of the first things I do is check their rate of speech. I ask them to bring a DVD or tape of one of their recent broadcasts so that I can count the number of words per minute at which they are speaking. I am not surprised anymore to find that many of them are speaking at rates close to 200 words per minute or even more! I also check the rate of speech of elementary school teachers, preachers, college professors, and others and find similar rates of somewhere in the vicinity of 180 to 190 words per minute. The typical rate is around 185 words per minute.

Our central nervous system (the auditory portion of our brain stem and brain along with the association areas of the brain that allow us to understand what people are saying) is designed to process and comprehend speech that is spoken at rates close to 128 words per minute. When listening to speech at that rate, we can more easily understand what speakers are saying to us.

Spoken speech is an extremely complex combination of voiced sounds, hisses, explosions, clicks, pauses, and inflections (the melody of speech). Some sounds of speech are silent, perhaps akin to "hisses"; others require the use of our voice, while others sound like guttural utterances. When speech is spoken at 180 to 190 words per minute, sentences are no longer sentences. They become a single elongated word, and the sounds of speech are distorted. So our central nervous system has difficulty accurately processing what it receives from our ears.

When speech is spoken at around 128 words per minute, the speaker begins to speak in whole words. All of the sounds necessary to pronounce words accurately are produced by the speaker, so speech becomes clearer and the probability of understanding what the speaker is saying is much greater. It is a wonderful experience!

What I am saying here is that when speech is produced at an all too typical rate of around 180 to 190 words per minute, it becomes nearly impossible to understand what is being said unless we exert some concentrated effort. For example, if I said at that rate "Do you want to have lunch?" It would probably resemble "Duyawanavlnch?" And if I combined other sentences with that one, we certainly would have difficulty keeping up with what was said!

What does that have to do with speaking to an audience? I always ask my audiences for whom I am giving a presentation about public speaking whether they remember Walter Cronkite or Tom Brokaw the news commentators. Viewers loved to watch them on television because they could easily understand what they were saying. The reason? Those two rehearsed speaking at a rate of approximately 126 to 130 words per minute during their broadcasts—very close to that of Fred Rogers of "Mr. Roger's Neighborhood" that young children loved when it was on the air. I don't think that Walter Cronkite and Tom Brokaw had studied the human central nervous system and rates of speech that it can comprehend. But somehow they must have surmised that a slower rate of speech would allow viewers to hear and understand what they were saying with greater ease. If you will notice, the well-known news commentators who have made it to the top of the rankings all speak at rates that are easy to understand. That is one of the reasons they became successful! Beside their personality and their presence in front of a camera, it was their manner of presentation that drew audiences to them. Enough said on that topic.

Gestures

As I said earlier, gestures can be an integral part of communication. It is an important aspect of non-verbal communication. Sometimes it is the only way to get a message across. For example, one day my wife, daughter, and I were in a noisy airport waiting area. I was trying to get their attention to tell them that they were at the wrong gate and to come to the correct one where I was standing. They were some distance away, standing in line at a coffee shop. I waved dramatically, trying to draw their attention to me. When my daughter happened to look my way I wildly signaled to her that both of them were to come to where I was standing because we only had a very few minutes before we were supposed to be on board! She then told my wife, and they both hurried to where I was standing. The level of noise was quite high and they were definitely out of shouting distance, so my wild gestures were the most efficient method of communicating at that moment.

Well, gesturing does help under those circumstances. However, on stage in front of an audience while speaking into a microphone, the use of gestures and the reasons for using them change rather dramatically. At the airport, the gestures that I used to get the attention of my daughter and my wife were, as I said above, rather dramatic. I was trying desperately to get their attention in a hurry! On stage, gestures take on a different complexion. They may be used to make a specific point or to point at something you want to draw attention to on the Power Point screen, but gestures are never overt, never overdone.

In the book that is authored by Jim Stovall and me entitled *The Art of Communication*, I referred to an example of what not to do. I said that last year I was asked to be a judge at a public speaking competition at a national convention. The competition is held each year to promote leadership skills among young adults. As I listened to each of the contestants, I rated them on various aspects of content and manner of presentation. At the appointed time, one young woman walked to the podium at the front of the room and began her speech. I noticed two things as she progressed through her twelve-minute speech. She was speaking, I am quite sure, at a rate of around 200 words per minute, and she was waving her arms wildly in multiples of directions! When her twelve minutes were up, I realized that I was becoming exhausted just listening to her.

When it was my turn to give my critique of her presentation, I told her that the primary thing that I learned from her speech was that she was evidently quite nervous! I told her in what I hoped to be a constructive manner that her rapid rate of speech and her unwieldly gestures were so distracting that I felt that I missed the content of her presentation. Her words were lost. She looked at me in what appeared to be disbelief.

The following are important to consider in regard to the use of gestures:

1. Do *not* overuse gestures. They can become distracting to the listener rather than constructive.

2. Avoid random gestures that add no direct meaning to what you are saying.

3. Overuse of gestures can indicate either a lack of confidence in what you are saying, lack of control, or that you are nervous.

4. Prudent use of gestures is the key, or not used *at all* unless they add to the content of what you are saying.

5. In the end, speaking with hands clasped in front of you a little under waist high, or loosely at your side is always appropriate. The audience will then be listening to *you* and will not spend their time watching your gestures.

As I asked earlier, have you watched a professional singer on stage? Those who possess the highest level of grace and professional demeanor stand with their hands at their sides, feet about 20 inches apart, and they use no gestures unless they add direct meaning to their song. In that way, the audience attends primarily to the singer's voice, their words, the expressions on their face, and the melody of the song. Nothing else is there to detract.

A Final Word Regarding Stage Presence

As public speakers, we can achieve the same level of professionalism as other respected speakers and singers when we speak. We can achieve what I call "grace" or perhaps an appearance of "serenity." We are doing nothing else to detract from what we are saying. All the listeners will attend to are the words that we are expressing, the use of our voice and the inflections that add meaning to what we are saying, our eyes and the contact that we have with the audience, and the movements of our head and shoulders, along with our manner of the presentation of *our self* to them. By using only our voice, expressive eye contact, and non-overt body language, we are demonstrating to the audience that we are speaking only to them. We are then speaking as professional presenters, not amateurs.

CHAPTER TEN

PRESENTATION PLATFORMS

By Jim Stovall

As we have stated previously, the most important part of any presentation is clearly defining the message. Once your message is boiled down to a single concept, then you have a myriad of options as to how to present your message. It is easy to become intimidated or discouraged when we see other people's presentations, particularly if their method is one that is not comfortable to us.

I am in the message business. The work I do in movies, television, books, radio, columns, and speeches represents different avenues and methodologies for presenting my message. It might appear that I have a wide variety of channels by which I present my message. While this might be true, there are many more methods of presenting that are not my strengths or chosen paths than the handful of methods I utilize.

My average speech runs approximately an hour and is generally delivered to thousands of people in an arena or a large convention center. Unless my audience connects with me after my presentation or reads my books, watches my movies or TV programs, follows my weekly columns, or listens to me on the radio, I may never have any further interaction with them.

My presentation to my normal audience is, therefore, a monologue. My audience hears from me, but I do not hear from them or even know who they are in the course of my presentation.

I have a talented colleague named Rebeka Graham whom I work with from time to time in some specialized presentations I do. Rebeka is predominantly a facilitator. Although she occasionally makes speeches to large groups of people, her talent and preferred presentation method revolves around workshops and small, interactive day-long or multi-day sessions. There are long portions of Rebeka's events in which the participants present the majority of the time.

I believe that in many cases the most valid information that people receive from a presentation is information they already had, but they have come to a new understanding of or perspective on.

One of the collaborations Rebeka and I present from time to time is based upon my book *Ultimate Productivity.* I wrote *Ultimate Productivity* in conjunction with Coach John Wooden, and the foreword was written by Steve Forbes. *Ultimate Productivity* deals with success through motivation, communication, and implementation.

Everyone has different preferences and styles in how they are motivated, best communicated with, and prefer to implement. These strengths or preferences are invariably reflected in how every individual would make a presentation. We developed a *Productivity Profile*—an online assessment—for people who read *The Ultimate Productivity* book or attend the events Rebeka and I present. If you and your colleagues or family members would like to take the *Productivity Profile* and get your own free assessment pertaining to your strengths and preferences in motivation, communication, and implementation, simply go to www.UltimateProductivity.com and use the access code 586404. This can be a powerful tool in developing your presentation style and in determining what type of presentation may be most impactful to your audience.

There are many ways to motivate people through your presentations. People are motivated by a myriad of factors including inspiration, causes, money, recognition, inclusion, and status. None of these are any more or less valid than the others, but if you're trying to motivate people using financial rewards when they are clearly attracted to causes and inspiration, you will likely fail. The way you communicate in presenting your message is critical, but it's not a one-size-fits-all proposition.

I have written 30 books to date with 10 million copies in print in several dozen languages. My columns are read by several million people each week throughout three continents, but I remain keenly aware that there are many people who will never be reached with my message via a written presentation. These people might, instead, watch one of my movies, listen to me on the radio, or attend one of my speaking engagements.

Implementation styles are also an important part of how you make a presentation. There are some people who are linear in how they learn while others need diversions, distractions, and multimedia input. There are some people who need to read about your message on a page or screen while others need to interact or have an experience.

Just as in motivation and communication, there are no right or wrong answers for everyone when it comes to implementation, but if you don't determine the appropriate format, your presentation can be doomed before it begins.

Almost 20 years ago, I was giving a speech in a magnificent outdoor amphitheater overlooking the ocean in Maui, Hawaii. One of the thousands of people in my audience that day was a gentleman named Brian Klemmer. Brian contacted me several weeks later and asked me to speak for 200 people who would be attending a weeklong event he was presenting known as *The Compassionate Samurai*.

I told Brian I was in the habit of speaking to thousands of people for approximately an hour at single-day events, and his weeklong workshop format didn't seem to fit my message or my mission. Brian explained to me that his audience was unique, and if I could impact them I could impact many multiple thousands of people because he told me people who attend *The Compassionate Samurai* events are influencers.

The theory is that there are people in the world who are compassionate. They have good hearts and benevolent intentions but often lack the resources to widely spread the good work they are committed to doing. Then there are other kinds of people who are like samurai warriors. They are powerful and influential but often do not have a focus on improving the world and benefiting everyone who lives in it.

Brian's *Compassionate Samurai* events were designed to bring these two groups of people together for a week of experiential presentations. Other than my opening speech, the majority of the weeklong presentation at *The Compassionate Samurai* events involve attendees experiencing the world and other people through a series of exercises.

This presentation involves diverse activity such as rock climbing, building a *Habitat for Humanity* house, going to a soup kitchen in an impoverished area, and other thought-provoking experiences.

Over the ensuing years, I have spoken at over 40 of the *Compassionate Samurai* events. They have expanded my presentation and given me the ability to extend my message in new and different ways.

My friend Brian Klemmer passed away several years ago, but his dedicated and talented team at Klemmer and Associates carry on his legacy and present weeklong *Compassionate Samurai* events several times each year.

All of us need to think about the legacy of our presentations. I'm a firm believer that when we learn something, we can change our lives; and when we teach something, we can change another person's life; but when we teach people to teach, we can change the world.

A great presenter remains aware of the fact that his message can be passed on by others and create a legacy of learning far beyond his or her life.

Your presentation platform and method will vary depending upon your audience. Each week, I do two radio broadcasts based upon my weekly syndicated column. One of the radio broadcasts goes out to dozens of stations throughout the country on the USA Network. The other radio broadcast is on a local station in my hometown.

On the national broadcast, I have to remember that my audience is massive and diverse. While we can discuss national or international issues of the day, I cannot refer to local weather, regional issues, or hometown politics on the nationwide radio broadcast; however, on the local radio broadcast in my hometown, we regularly talk about the road conditions in our city, local sports teams, and weather conditions. Understanding and remembering the makeup of your audience is an ongoing part of every presentation.

My books have been translated into dozens of languages and distributed throughout the world. I regularly hear from readers who live in countries that I had literally never heard of before they contacted me.

Periodically, I interact with the talented professionals who translate my books into various languages. I am constantly reminded that just because you translate into a language does not mean you have translated your message into another culture. I remember writing about a character in one of my books, and I described him as "having a tiger by the tail." While this phrase may be familiar and descriptive to people in North America, I learned from a Mandarin translator who called me from China that she and all of my Chinese readers would have no clear understanding of having a tiger by the tail. In fact, she informed me that many of my readers throughout Asia for whom she would be translating were located in areas where tigers are indigenous, and those readers would have a quite different understanding of having a tiger by the tail than my American audience.

Presentations remain the process of transporting the message in your mind to the minds of your audience. The fewer barriers, transfers, and impediments involved in this process, the better your presentation will be received.

The talented young lady who translated that book into Mandarin Chinese became as much a part of that presentation as I am to my readers in Asia. Some people's presentations are singular, but most often a presentation involves a collaboration.

My book *The Ultimate Life* was turned into a movie that was directed by Michael Landon, Jr. People throughout the last half of the twentieth century knew his father, Michael Landon, Sr., as the star of several popular and long-running television series. Michael Landon, Sr. presented his message each week to television audiences around the world in collaboration with the other cast members involved in the series. Michael Landon, Jr. focuses his presentation skills on being a director and working behind the camera. While his performance may not be as readily apparent, it is just as important if not more important than the performance of the actors whom he directs.

Quality collaborations are an invaluable element of most presentations. It might seem that you are simply reading words on the page that I have written, and the only people involved in this presentation are me and you as the presenter and audience. Nothing could be further from the truth.

As a blind person, I cannot read printed pages, and I have never learned how to type. These words you are reading and all of the words in my 30 books, one thousand newspaper columns, and various screenplays are dictated to my talented colleague Dorothy Thompson. Dorothy remains among the best editors and grammarians in the publishing industry. The words you are reading would never have been typed or printed without Dorothy's involvement in my presentation.

Furthermore, the book you are holding is also a presentation of my esteemed coauthor, Dr. Ray Hull. Our combined work in this volume was brought to life first by our mutual colleague and friend at the U.S. Department of Education, Jo Ann McCann. Jo Ann had the insight to see that putting Ray and me together could result in one plus one equals ten. Then this book became a reality because of my publisher Dave Wildasin and his talented team at Sound Wisdom Publishing. The involvement of printers, truckers, warehouse people, bookstore employees, and others brought this book to you.

When it comes to presenting, the words of the great poet John Donne, "No man is an island," are one hundred percent true.

Your conviction, passion, and energy will always be a part of your presentation regardless of the platform you utilize. People will be more attracted to your message and embrace it based on the height of your emotion as opposed to the depth of your knowledge. The old adage that "people don't care how much you know until they know how much you care" will apply to every formal, informal, or casual presentation you make.

Emotion and passion can be delivered in a number of ways. Powerful lines, memorable quotes, and poignant poetry can indelibly and impactfully deliver your message to your audience. While you always want to have high energy, enthusiasm, and emotion as a part of your presentation, never forget that silence can be as persuasive as any oration.

I have worked with the esteemed actor Brian Dennehy in two of the movies based on my novels. Many actors try to lobby or encourage a movie's writers or director to give them more lines than the script originally called for. Brian, on the other hand, often will ask a director if he can leave out lines, preferring to make his presentation nonverbally. Some of the best movie scenes involving Brian Dennehy have little or no dialogue. What you don't say and how you don't say it can be as impactful as anything you might say.

Throughout recorded history, many of the most powerful and enduring presentations involved storytelling. Storytelling is both an art and a science. Powerfully delivered stories can both compress and maximize your presentation. A presenter can struggle through many points over a long period of time trying to express a concept, or they might simply refer to Jack and the Beanstalk, *It's a Wonderful Life*, The Good Samaritan, or *Rocky*. The mere mention of a powerful story that has become a part of our culture can take your audience to a different time and place and impactfully deliver an emotional message.

The most powerful stories are your own. Great presenters develop signature stories that permanently connect them with their audience in much the same way that enduring hit songs connect singers with their fans.

I have paid huge amounts of money and stood in long lines to go to a concert in order to hear one of my favorite performers sing a song that is in my own album collection at home. It's not about the song. It's about the experience.

One of my signature stories that I utilize in virtually every speech is about a young boy name

d Christopher. If you want to experience the Christopher story, you can see it as a part of a video from one of my arena speeches by going to www.JimStovall.com. I have met people who have traveled great distances and sat in my audience multiple times to hear the Christopher story again or share it with friends and family members they brought to my events.

As described earlier, you must put yourself in the picture when you're creating an impactful story to be a part of your presentation. Your audience is much more willing to allow you to give them your message when you give them a part of yourself. Just as we more readily accept advice or recommendations from people we know, people will embrace your presentation if they feel like they know you.

Vulnerability, authenticity, and transparency should be a part of every presentation. People will be comfortable with what you say as soon as they are comfortable with who you are.

CHAPTER ELEVEN

THE ART OF CONCLUDING YOUR PRESENTATION: MAKING AN IMPACT!

By Ray Hull, PhD

I was reading one of my favorite publications the other day, the 2015 edition of "The Old Farmer's Almanac." As one tracks the months of the year in that old and well-loved journal, there are quotes and other sayings that I look forward to reading throughout the highlights that are written about each month of the year. One saying caught my eye the other day as I was going through the month of November. It said, paraphrased, "A strong beginning is good, but a great ending is even better!" I think that the unknown author was actually referring to life, but I almost immediately related it to public presentations. A good beginning to your presentation is important in order to grab the attention of your audience. But an even better ending will give the audience something to remember—to remember you and your message!

A few days after your presentation, they will probably not remember how it began, but if you give them something in your concluding statements that makes an impact, then that is what they will remember and perhaps tell others. So the rule is—what you say last will be remembered best!

Great Endings: What Not to Do

Let's begin a discussion of great endings with some thoughts on what *not* to do when concluding your presentation. Sometimes it is better to learn how *not* to do something before learning how to do it *correctly*. Andrew Bradbury in his book *Successful Presentation Skills*[1] gives four common errors that can occur when one comes to the conclusion of a presentation:

1. *The Emergency Stop!*

Without warning, the speaker comes to an abrupt stop and says something such as, "Well, I think that's about all I have to say, so I'll stop there," and sits down. How can a speaker "think" that she or he has nothing more to say? Did the speaker not previously know that there is nothing more to say? If something was left out, the audience will never know! It should never be necessary to tell the audience that you have come to the end of your presentation. It should be evident by the way you have reached closure and made your final "inspirational" statements.

By briefly rephrasing the points that you have made during the presentation and then giving a final statement that you want the audience to remember, you have then concluded! There is absolutely *no* reason to say something like, "Well...I guess that's all." The fact that you have concluded your speech should be self-evident and should make an impact! Then you can sit down while listening to the loud applause!

2. *The Endless Maze Speaker*

The "endless maze" speaker can be recognized by the way that she or he ends their presentation about as lost and confused as the audience. The speaker may say something like, "And so I'll conclude on that point—and remind you of the comment I made earlier about...."

And off the speaker goes again, apparently lost and trying to find a way out of the maze of the presentation by continuing on without arriving at a point where giving a concluding statement can appropriately be made! The speaker is obviously not working from a well-prepared script and hopes that if she or he talks long enough all of the details of what was intended to be said will sooner or later find their way into the presentation. By that time, if it ever arrives, the audience will probably be asleep!

3. *The Clichéd Climax*

Unlike the emergency stop, whereby the speaker seems to arrive at the ending of the presentation by accident, the "clichéd climax" presenter obviously knows when she is going to finish and insists on broadcasting the fact. Conclusions such as, "In conclusion, here is what I came to say…" (Doesn't the audience already know what she came to say?) or "Just before I leave, I want to say…" or "And finally… (Does that mean you are happy that you are about done?) or "And I'd like to leave you with this final thought…."

It is as though the speaker wants to prepare us for that "awful" moment when she or he will stop speaking! Ugh!

4. *The More the Merrier*

Unlike the "endless maze" speaker, where the presenter keeps harking back to earlier comments and regurgitates them in so many words, when a "more the merrier" speaker reaches the end of a presentation, it is not an ending after all but rather a new beginning! The process of summing up his ideas seems to generate a whole new series of thoughts that weren't there before!

However, as Bradbury kindly states, the audience may not have the patience or the endurance to continue listening to what appears to be a new presentation that is found to be within the original presentation! Last-minute ideas, no matter how brilliant, should be saved for another day. The only way that those new ideas might be appropriate is if they are absolutely essential to the other points you were making!

Know When to Stop!

Our church once had a pastor who would continue to give his sermon until the digital clock in front of the choir where I sat was straight up and down 12:00 noon, the time when the service was to conclude. Our choir would sing the closing doxology and then, thinking the service was over, would begin picking up our music folders and other odds and ends, ready to leave. However, the pastor would again walk to the altar and begin to give closing remarks, usually adding a new text and an additional message to what he had previously said during his lengthy sermon! The congregation would re-seat themselves out of respect for the pastor and wait patiently while he continued to add new information to what he had already said during his sermon.

We supposed that he wanted to make sure that we received his message, or perhaps he thought that his original sermon hadn't made enough of an impact. But the previously mentioned "more the merrier" add-on generally turned out to be a new mini-sermon that was a continuation of his previous sermon, and we would wonder if he was ever going to stop talking! Later that year, we thankfully received word that he would soon move to another parish!

A Successful Finish to Your Presentation

Remember, audiences have "sitting limitations." That is, they can only sit and be attentive for a limited period of time. For college-age students, it has been found that 20 minutes is the maximum amount of time during which one can expect to gain and hold their attention for purposes of learning new material.

We all have sitting limitations. The pastor referred to above seemed to have little sensitivity to the sitting limitations of the congregation. After an hour and a half, many were squirming in their seats because they had bathroom needs. Others were getting sore bottoms from sitting on hard wooden pews, and they needed to stand up for relief. Most had stopped listening 40 minutes prior to the time he concluded his sermon! He seemed to have no concept of the duration limits of an audience!

Be Aware of Your Audience's Sitting Limitations

To be assured that your audience is still alert and ready to receive the close of your presentation, you must be aware of their limitations. *And it is also refreshing to know that few presentations fail because they ended early!*

If you can say everything you wanted to say in less than your allotted time, consider it a bonus. The audience will! Don't try to pad your speech just because you have not used up all of the time you were allotted. By concluding your presentation meaningfully in less than the time that was given to you, the audience will probably remember you and your presentation fondly!

Make It a Memorable Ending

Toogood[2] gives some sound pointers on ways to conclude your presentation in such a way that it is memorable and will leave a lasting impression:

1. *Summarize Your Key Points*

Summarize with perhaps one or at the most three main points. This means that you can restate your main message, then perhaps give one or three reasons or sub-themes to back it up. Or simply restate your main theme and forget about the sub-themes. The best rule of thumb is to stick with one main message and leave it at that! You can restate it in other words, but you are still stressing your original theme. For example: "So our future, as you can see, lies in our own hands. It is not too late to correct our mistakes and to recognize that our success will depend on...."

2. *Loop Back to the Beginning*

Similar to the suggestion above, one of the best concluding statements involves letting your ending echo the beginning of your presentation. This technique is not only intellectually satisfying but also in a design sense aesthetically pleasing. And it can also save time in preparation. That is because once you figure out what your theme is for the presentation and you can synthesize that theme into simple but assertive language, then your theme can become not only your *bottom line* (your last words) but also your *headline* (your first words). So you can reach back to your beginning and pull up the personal story, illustration, quotation, or rhetorical question and emphasize your initial point as you conclude your presentation. If it's a story, don't tell it in exactly the same way during your conclusion. But retell it by reminding the audience of that little boy, that old man and his bit of philosophy, or the story of yourself when, with stars in your eyes, you began your career!

3. *Ask the Audience to Do Something*

If you are giving a speech with the intent to inspire action by members of the audience, you might ask them to go out and spread the good news! Or, if you are the senior corporate officer of a large company and are chairing a meeting of employees who are competing with each other within the same company, you might challenge them in the name of cooperation and ask for consensus. If you are requesting support for a civic project, you might ask for help, endorsement, ideas, cooperation, or donations! You are inspiring your audience to move forward in support of your efforts on behalf of your community. You are asking members of the audience to do something, and that is the motivation for your presentation.

4. Tell a Story That Embraces Your Theme

We are cautioned regarding this tactic for a conclusion to your presentation. Telling a story, if not done well, may hinder more than help. A story has to be told with conviction, not self-consciously or without feeling. If you use a story to close a presentation, it must be one that hits the mark exactly, doesn't take too long to tell, and makes a clear statement that will move an audience in such a way that it will strike an emotional chord in them.

When the story has concluded, the most important thing for you to do is to sit down and be quiet. If there is applause, it will happen without your standing and appearing to beg. Adding a finish—after a story has been told that stirs the emotions of the audience—will subtract from its impact. Your purpose is to give your audience something that they will remember six weeks from the time you concluded your presentation. By telling stories and painting pictures for your audience, you are giving them something to take with them, and that they will remember. Just remember to do it well. If you are not a good actor, you may not want to try the story finish.

End with a Purpose!

Timothy Koegel[3] in his book entitled *The Exceptional Presenter* emphasizes what I said earlier in this chapter, "What you say last will be remembered best." We begin our presentations with a *purpose*, and we can conclude our presentation with a restatement of our purpose but perhaps in slightly different words. That tactic can conclude a presentation effectively.

Because the purpose statement may provide one, two, or three key points that you want your audience to remember, concluding with the same key points can give them what you want them to take home with them. Use your *purpose* statement to hammer home your key points one final time. For example, something like, "If there are no further questions, keep in mind that the destiny of this organization is not a matter of chance, it is a matter of choice! The choices we make in the next few weeks will…" is a wonderful way to conclude your presentation. The point or points that you want the audience to remember are the ones that conclude your remarks.

"Keep in mind that 90 percent of what you say in the body of your presentation will be forgotten by the end of the day."[4] Make sure that your conclusion stays with your audience and is not forgotten. It may very well be the most powerful component of what you say!

Additional Avenues for a Successful Conclusion

Bradbury gives us some additional suggestions on making a suitable closing for your presentation.[5] He refers to the following:

The Challenge

Give your audience a challenge to address a problem! Couch the challenge in terms of what we can do or will do, *not* what we *should* do. "Should do" refers to something that we might do if we have time, not that we absolutely need to do it now or even later. A mere emotional appeal for some action may be rousing to the audience, but it is likely to lead to nothing in regard to action.

The Call to Action

In regard to a call to action rather than a challenge, it may be better to use persuasion to make your point. Your concluding statements may then be more effective if you confine them to the points in favor of a proposal and then end with a description of the next steps that those in the audience are to take. You have probably already covered the contradictory arguments during your presentation, so there is no reason to reiterate them in your concluding statements. The author uses an example of a strong call to action that was used as the climax of a political rally, when the party leader challenged his followers, "Go home and prepare to live successfully!" And the challenge was found to be successful.

The Feel Good Factor

Motivational speakers aim to leave the audience with a warm glow rather than proposing some other course of action. Of course the "feel good" conclusion proposed here would not be appropriate in something like a press conference or a political rally.

The three most popular forms of a feel good ending make use of a quotation or a piece of poetry or a story that has a happy ending. In all cases, according to Bradbury, the material should be short and to the point. As long as the material is highly emotionally charged, the precise nature of the quotation or poem or story will be determined by the emotional response you wish to arouse in your audience. However, it should be dictated by the content of the presentation in order to solidify the points you were making. Again, give the audience something they can take away with them and remember you by.

Remember the Red Light

When the "red light" goes on, then be ready to conclude your presentation. The red light doesn't have to be an actual red light, but it should be implanted indelibly in your mind and your watch! When that red light comes on, don't look startled. You should have at least two possible conclusions to your presentation—one that you present at your leisure, and one to present when the red light goes on! If you plan your presentation in such a way that you can conclude your presentation at your leisure, then there is no problem. If you have to end your presentation in 45 seconds, then you need an alternative—something short and sweet. Perhaps not "sweet" in relation to sweet and sugary but something catchy and thought provoking. Or a challenge to your audience that will move them to action.

Any concluding remarks should take no longer than two to three minutes. Otherwise, the audience may compare you to that pastor I referred to earlier in this chapter. A statement that will conclude what you came to say and offer a thought-provoking challenge or offer the audience a bit of advice that they can take with them can do wonders. It will do more to cause an audience to remember you and your presentation fondly than a conclusion that does not seem to end or seems to have little to do with what your presentation contained.

A Final Word to the Wise Presenter

Most of all, when you are concluding your presentation walk to the front of the stage and talk directly to members of the audience. Look directly at as many as you can, and speak conversationally to them, not dogmatically nor in an overly dramatic manner. By conversationally, I mean to speak to them as though you are carrying on a personal conversation with each of the members of the audience. They will remember you as a personable and honest presenter—a personable and honest person whom they look forward to hearing speak again.

Notes

1. Bradbury, *Successful Presentation Skills.*

2. Toogood, *The Articulate Executive.*

3. Koegel, *The Exceptional Presenter.*

4. Ibid.

5. Bradbury, *Successful Presentation Skills.*

CHAPTER TWELVE

PRESENTATIONS, POSSIBILITIES, AND POTENTIAL

By Jim Stovall

I'm a firm believer that success in life is not as much a result of knowing all the answers but, instead, of asking the right questions.

Coach John Wooden encouraged me before undertaking any task, job, or presentation to ask myself one simple question. "What would I do right now if I were amazing?"

Asking yourself this question before every phone call, meeting, confrontation, task, or presentation will revolutionize both your personal and your professional life. If you discover you are preparing to undertake a task that doesn't require you to be amazing or doesn't warrant that much effort, you may want to reconsider whether that particular task is worthy of your time and effort.

In this book, we have offered a number of concepts, tips, and suggestions as to how you can be a better presenter in your life. Some people will become professional speakers, trainers, or presenters, while others will simply use their presentation skills as a part of their regular routine.

It would be hard to imagine the career path, job description, or family dynamic that did not require presentations. In our world here in the twenty-first century, we are all connected in new and dynamic ways. These connections create the reality that we may work with or have personal relationships with people we have yet to meet. There are people I have done business with for years whom I have never met in person. We evaluated one another, negotiated, and determined to form a business relationship all based upon our presentations.

In the presentation world, perception becomes reality. It doesn't matter how great you may be. People will judge your presentation.

If you are one of the special individuals who has decided to take presentations beyond your personal and family life and even beyond a tool in your career and you have decided to become a professional speaker or presenter, I want to welcome you to an exciting and dynamic profession.

I was not aware of the speaking profession as a career path until I stumbled into it. Then I learned that there are over 7,000 paid presentations every day. That was a staggering statistic 25 years ago when I entered the speaking profession, and while it still astounds me I found it to be true. If you're going to be a professional speaker, you need to make a quality presentation about your speech and your topic.

As a professional speaker or presenter, you will learn that you get paid for getting booked more than for giving the speech itself. You may be tempted to contact speakers bureaus, and while I would encourage you to do this you cannot depend on speakers bureaus to book you until you've already had some success on your own. It's a bit like banks not wanting to loan you money until you really don't need it.

I would encourage you to reach out to speakers and presenters you respect and review their promotional material and overall marketing presentation.

I never like to take advice from someone who doesn't have what I want. Shortly after you declare your intent to become a professional speaker, you will find that there are countless individuals and organizations who want to charge you considerable sums of money to put together your promotional material, market your speeches, or promote your career in some way. You should be very cautious and skeptical as many of these pitches are designed to separate you from your hard-earned money.

When presenting yourself as a professional speaker, it is critical that you have a clear and concise topic or message that you offer to meeting planners, promoters, and event coordinators. These professionals are results-oriented. They will be judging what benefits will be derived by the people who hear your presentation that can be translated into successful results.

Whenever possible, it is best to have someone presenting you as a speaker. I consider myself a very good marketer and salesperson. I feel comfortable sharing the positive benefits of almost any product or service except for me and my speeches.

Imagine yourself calling to inquire about booking a top-rated recording artist, actor, or other spotlight performer. You would not expect for them to answer the phone themselves and discuss the benefits of hiring them.

For over 20 years, I have been privileged to have one of the best marketing directors in the speaking industry. Kelly Morrison is a true professional in our industry and a great presenter herself. She positions me perfectly with the people to whom I am going to be speaking so that we all know what to expect.

An important part of the speaking and presenting business is known as the "back-of-the-room" sales. This involves offering your books, videos, and other support material that build upon your message either at the venue or at a later point in time. Beth Sharp is a great professional who works in our office. She handles all the calls and inquiries from people or organizations that want to find out about getting any of my 30 books, various movies, speaking videos, or other products. If you want to find out how good she is or learn more about our other resources that can help you with your presentation and beyond, just call Beth Sharp at 918-627-1000.

For over 20 years, I have written a weekly syndicated column that appears in newspapers, magazines, and online publications around the world. If you would like to receive this column via email each week, just request it at Jim@JimStovall.com.

Occasionally, I write an article for a specific industry or professional publication. Recently, I wrote an article for meeting professionals and event planners in one of their industry publications. In this article, I called on my 20 years of experience on the road making speeches to countless types of groups. The article was entitled "Help Me Help You" and informed professionals in the industry how they could help speakers like me to create more value for them and the people who attend their events when they hire me.

I provided the ten tips below in that article. You may want to use some of them or adapt the list for your presenting business.

1. Tell the speaker or presenter what it is you want to accomplish with your meeting or their time onstage, not what you want them to do. I have given well over 1,000 speeches to several million people throughout the years. Meeting professionals regularly tell me what they want me to do, but when I ask what they want to accomplish there is often a better suggestion I can make born out of the countless experiences I have had over the years. You know your people and your organization, and I know my presentation and how to get the best results. Let's plan, coordinate, and cooperate.

2. I and every professional who will ever present to your organization or meeting should provide you with a pre-prepared, quality introduction. If the master of ceremonies or whoever is doing the introduction wants to add comments, background info, or other specific details, they should do it before the prepared intro, therefore bringing the presenter onto the stage immediately after the standard introduction. This provides the context and the continuity we need to give you the results you want.

3. As a blind person myself, I always need a walkthrough onstage at the venue any time

before the meeting. This allows me to orient myself and be ready to walk onto the stage independently; however, you should offer a similar opportunity and a sound check to every presenter you work with.

4. Tell your speaker or presenter what time you want them to end their presentation, not how long you want them to be onstage. Programs often run long or short, and a good speaker will get you back on schedule if you provide them with this simple information.

5. Always share with your speaker what will be preceding them on the agenda at your event and what will be following them. I have been introduced immediately after a moment of silence being observed for the passing of the founder of a corporation, and I have been introduced right after an exuberant celebration announcing an organization's meeting and exceeding their annual goal. I can deal with either circumstance, but they each require a different approach.

6. I am willing to do virtually anything for a client between the time I arrive at the venue and the time I leave; however, casual meet-and-greet sessions before the event often take

away from the "wow" factor you are paying for.

7. Update your speaker on any major corporate or association news that may occur right up until your speaker walks onstage. If there is new legislation, a labor strike, a merger, or a technological breakthrough that impacts your people, it should impact your speaker.

8. Make sure your presenter knows what speakers you had last week, last month, or last year and how they were received. Great speakers know each other and can adjust accordingly.

9. Provide every speaker or presenter with emergency contact info and backup for the key people at your event. Get all the similar information from your presenter. You can't collaborate if you can't get hold of one another.

10. Provide your speaker or presenter with evaluations and follow-up feedback. It will help them to help the next group they serve.

Promoting yourself as a speaker, getting booked, and dealing with all the details surrounding the event are critical, but they are only the fundamentals that set the stage for your presentation. As my late, great friend and mentor

Dr. Stephen Covey often said, "You've got to begin with the end in mind."

The second you walk onstage, you leave all the promotional and prep work behind you and enter into the world of your presentation. Regardless of whether your message is emotional or academic, you want to make it transformational. You must be committed to the proposition that your audience will be different when you leave the stage than they were when you were introduced.

Doing something memorable is a great way to hammer home your message so it will stay with your audience for a lifetime. Great stories, memorable quotes, poignant poems, and humorous stage antics are all tools that a great presenter can use to empower their message. Don't be afraid to tell your audience what you are going to tell them before you deliver your message, and don't be afraid to remind them what you told them when you end the presentation.

Leave your audience with a connection. It needs to be some hook that will bring them back to the transformational time and place within your presentation. My hooks involve a signature story, several power quotes, an emotional poem, and my contact info. I want my live audiences, as well as you reading this book, to know that the end of this presentation is not the end of our relationship.

Any time you need help, encouragement, or direction, just reach out to me at Jim@JimStovall.com. I am serious about you succeeding, both in your personal and professional life, using your innate presentation skills and the tools and techniques in this book.

Becoming a great professional speaker or presenter will bring you much fame and fortune. I believe any such benefit comes with a corresponding responsibility. For this reason, I made the commitment many years ago to make a free speech for every one I get paid to do. Most of my *pro bono* presentations are done in my hometown where you may find me in an elementary school, nursing home, or raising money for a nonprofit organization.

As stated in an earlier chapter, life is about finding your gift and giving it away. Nowhere is this more true than in the world of speaking and presenting.

I have had the privilege of sharing the stage with many of the great luminaries in the speaking profession. These gifted individuals have become my mentors and my friends. I would consider it an honor and a privilege to share the stage with you someday. I am looking forward to your success as a presenter, a professional, and a person.

I have a special poem I use to close and punctuate my speeches. This poem shares a special message that I want to leave with my audiences, and now I want to leave that message with you.

Hold on to your dreams and stand tall
Even when those around you

would force you to crawl.
Hold on to your dreams as a race you must run
Even when reality whispers, "You'll never be done."
Hold on to your dreams
And wait for the miracles to come
Because on that magical day,
Your dreams and your reality will merge into one.

ABOUT RAY HULL, PHD

Ray Hull, PhD is Professor of Communication Sciences and Disorders and Coordinator of the Doctor of Audiology Program3, College of Health Professions, Wichita State University. He was Chair of the Department of Communication Disorders, University of Northern Colorado for twelve years; held administrative posts within the graduate school, being responsible for graduate program review and evaluation both at UNC and Wichita State University for eight years; was the Director of Planning and Budget for the Office of the President for seven successful years at the University of Northern Colorado, responsible for the allocation of over $60 million in state appropriated funds; has held administrative posts both at the University of Northern Colorado in the College of Health and Human Sciences, the Office of the President, and at Wichita State University through the Graduate School; and is a successful grants person, with over $12 million in competitively funded federal grants.

Background

His background in the fields of communication disorders and the neuroscience of human communication began with his college degree in public speaking, drama, and radio/television broadcast, and then moved into graduate work in disorders of human communication, and then a doctorate in the neurosciences of human communication that involved a combined doctoral degree from the University of Colorado School of Medicine and the University of Denver. He works extensively in coaching and speaking on the art of interpersonal communication in professional life—the nature of interpersonal communication that supports success in one's professional life.

Dr. Hull is past Chair of the ASHA Committee on Communication Problems of the Aging; a past member of the Committee on Governmental Regulations; a member of the ASHA/ETS National Audiology Praxis Advisory Committee; the ASHA Advisory Committee for the project "Upgrading Services to Communicatively Impaired Persons," Bureau of Health Professions; the Advisory,

Guidance, and Evaluation Team of the ASHA Project on Satellite Training on Communicative Behavior of Older Americans, Administration on Aging; Vice Chair of the ASHA Audiology Advisory Counsel; member of the ASHA Audiology Advisory Counsel; among other national and state association appointments as found in his CV.

He is or has been consultant and advisor to numerous federal agencies, including the Bureau of Health Professions, DHHS; the National Institute on Aging, PHS; the National Institute of Mental Health, NIH; the Administration on Aging, DHHS; the U.S. Department of Education, Office of Special Education and Rehabilitative Services. He has also been an advisor to Congress, the U.S. House of Representatives Select Committee on Health, Sub-Committee on Health and Long-Term Care; the U.S. Senate Special Committee on Aging and their Committee on Health, Education, Labor, and Pensions in the areas of health services delivery and disability issues; and the U.S. Senate Small Business Innovation Research Program. He is advisor to the Health Care Financing Administration, DHHS on health and mental health issues. He was also selected by the Bureau of Health Professions, HRSA, DHHS to represent the field of aging on their Council on Disability Rehabilitation. Further, he is advisor to the Bureau of Health Professions, PHS; Health Careers Opportunity Program; and advisor/panelist to the Office of Minority Health, PHS, DHHS; and the Division of Allied Health, BHP, HRSA, DHHS; he has been advisor to the World Health Organization on aging issues; advisor/panelist to the various grants programs of the Office of Special Education Programs (OSEP) of the Office of Special Education and Rehabilitative Services (OSERS); U.S. Department of Education as a member of their standing panel for twenty years prior to an additional three-year term including OSEP, NIDRR and RSA; was a member of the Scientific Merit Review Board of the Veterans Administration Health Services Research and Development Program; and is a current grants panelist for Health Resources and Services Administration, DHHS. He is currently advisor to the Smithsonian Institution, Washington, D.C. on behalf of their Accessibility Program for Children and Adults with Disabilities, and is narrator for the Smithsonian magazine. He is also currently an advisor/consultant on behalf of the American Institute for Research, Washington, D.C.

Dr. Hull has been editorial advisor to the *American Journal of Audiology, Ear and Hearing, The Journal of the American Auditory Society, The Journal of the American Academy of Audiology*, the *Journal of International Audiology*, and numerous book publishing companies.

He is sought after as a speaker/presenter and has authored and presented over 300 presentations and workshops across the U.S., Canada, South America, and Europe on the art of communication in professional practice, environmental design, central auditory processing, and hearing rehabilitation for children and adults with impaired hearing. These workshops have as their basis the diagnostic and neurophysiologic aspects of auditory impairment, central auditory processing in adulthood and aging, its physiology and psycho/social impact, techniques for counseling and rehabilitation of those persons, the art and science of grant proposal writing, and the art of interpersonal communication and persuasion in professional practice.

His books include:

- *Hearing Impairment Among Aging Persons*, published by Sage Publications, Beverly Hills, California

- Rehabilitative Audiology: Part I—The Adult, and Part II—The Elderly Client, published by Grune and Stratton, Inc., New York

- *Communication Disorders In Aging*, published by Sage Publications, Beverly Hills, California

- He was the invited author of the monograph entitled *The Communicatively Impaired Elderly*, for Seminars in Speech, Language and Hearing, Thieme-Stratton Pub. Co.

- *The Hearing Impaired Child In School* published by Grune and Stratton, New York

- Aural Rehabilitation: Serving Hearing Impaired Children and Adults was published by Singular Publishing Group, San Diego

- *Aural Rehabilitation* published by Chapman-Hall Publishing Co., London

- *Hearing in Aging* Singular Publishing Group

- Aural Rehabilitation—The Elements and Process For Serving Hearing Impaired Children and Adults published by Thomson Publishing, New York, 2002

- *Introduction to Aural Rehabilitation*, Plural Publishing, San Diego, 2010

- *Hearing and Aging,* Plural Publishing, 2011

Dr. Hull is the recipient of numerous honors and awards. He was elected Fellow of the American Speech-Language-Hearing Association. He was awarded the Red River Award by the Manitoba Ministry of Health and the Winnipeg League for the Hard of Hearing, Winnipeg, Manitoba, for significant service on behalf of hearing-impaired older adults. He was named the University Distinguished Scholar at the University of Northern Colorado. He was named Distinguished Pioneer in Gerontology by the Colorado Gerontological Society. He was awarded the Public Health Service Award, U.S. Public Health Service, PHS, DHSS for significant service to PHS, Region VIII for research and service on behalf of hearing-impaired older adults. He was also named Distinguished Scholar of the College of Health and Human Services, University of Northern Colorado. He was awarded the Faculty Achievement Award, College of Health and Human Sciences, University of Northern Colorado, for outstanding scholarly activity and teaching excellence. He was also awarded the Award of Excellence for Outstanding Public Leadership in the Cause of Better Hearing and Speech. He was again named Distinguished Scholar of the College of Health and Human Sciences, University of Northern Colorado, and was awarded the Outstanding Faculty Achievement Award. He received the Distinguished Professor Award at Wichita State University by the University chapter of Mortar Board. He was also awarded the Wichita State University College of Education Teaching Award for Excellence in Teaching and the Emery Lindquist Faculty Award for Scholarship and Teaching. He was awarded the 2001 and the 2006 Professor Incentive Award, Wichita State University.

In 2002, 2003, 2004, 2005, and 2007 he was named to *Who's Who Among America's Educators*. In 2009, he received the President's Distinguished Service Award at Wichita State University. He received the Rodenberg Award for Excellence in Teaching by the Wichita State University College of Health Professions in 2014.

Dr. Hull was educated at McPherson College with a B.A. degree in Forensics, Drama, and Mass

Communication; University of South Dakota with the M.A. in Communication and Communication Disorders; and the University of Denver, School of Communication with the PhD in Audiology/Neurosciences. He is an active member of the American Speech-Language-Hearing Association, the Academy of Rehabilitative Audiology, and the American Academy of Audiology, and holds ASHA Certification both in Audiology and Speech-Language Pathology. He is Fellow of both the American Speech-Language-Hearing Association and the American Academy of Audiology.

ABOUT JIM STOVALL

In spite of blindness, Jim Stovall has been a National Olympic weightlifting champion, a successful investment broker, the president of the Emmy Award-winning Narrative Television Network, and a highly sought-after author and platform speaker. He is the author of 30 books, including the best seller, *The Ultimate Gift*, which is now a major motion picture from 20th Century Fox starring James Garner and Abigail Breslin. Three of his other novels have also been made into movies with two more in production.

Steve Forbes, president and CEO of *Forbes* magazine, says, "Jim Stovall is one of the most extraordinary men of our era."

For his work in making television accessible to our nation's 13 million blind and visually impaired people, the President's Committee on Equal Opportunity selected Jim Stovall as the Entrepreneur of the Year. Jim Stovall has been featured in *The Wall Street Journal, Forbes* magazine, *USA Today*, and has been seen on *Good Morning America, CNN,* and *CBS Evening News.* He was also chosen as the International Humanitarian of the Year, joining Jimmy Carter, Nancy Reagan, and Mother Teresa as recipients of this honor.

Jim Stovall can be reached at 918-627-1000 or Jim@JimStovall.com.

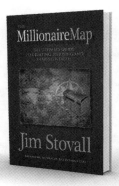